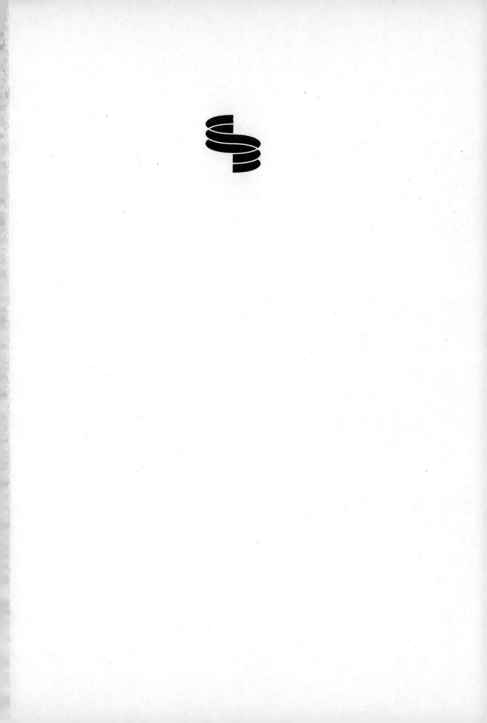

ALSO BY DR. BOB ROTELLA

BOOKS

Golf Is Not a Game of Perfect
Golf Is a Game of Confidence
The Golf of Your Dreams
Life Is Not a Game of Perfect

AUDIOTAPES

Playing to Win—Golf, Business, Life
Golfing Out of Your Mind
Putting Out of Your Mind
Focusing Your Mind for Competition

VIDEOTAPE

Putt to Win (with Brad Faxon)

Putting Out of Your Mind

DR. BOB ROTELLA

with Bob Cullen

SIMON & SCHUSTER SOURCE

New York • London • Toronto

Sydney

SIMON & SCHUSTER SOURCE
Rockefeller Center
1230 Avenue of the Americas
New York, NY 10020

Copyright © 2001 by Robert J. Rotella
All rights reserved,
including the right of reproduction
in whole or in part in any form.
SIMON & SCHUSTER Source and colophon
are registered trademarks of Simon & Schuster, Inc.
Manufactured in the United States of America

10 9 8 7

Library of Congress Cataloging-in-Publication Data
is available
ISBN 0-7432-1213-4

I dedicate this book to the people at *Golf Digest* and *Golf Digest* schools who, in 1979, gave me my first chance to work with golfers and learn from them. They have my thanks for their help, inspiration, and support.

From the magazine: Jerry Tarde, Bob Carney, and Mike Stachura.

From the schools: Bob Toski, Jim Flick, Davis Love Jr., Peter Kostis, Hank Johnson, Jack Lumpkin, Dr. Dee Dee Owens, Dick Aultman, Dick Drager, John Elliott, Charlie Epps, and Chuck Cook.

And special thanks to the first panel of the *Golf Digest* schools' advisory board with whom I worked: Sam Snead, Paul Runyan, and Dr. Cary Middlecoff.

This book is dedicated as well to all the players on the PGA, LPGA, and Senior PGA tours who have allowed me the opportunity to coach their minds and their attitudes. Some of them are mentioned in its pages. All of them have my thanks.

Contents

Introduction

by Brad Faxon

WHEN I FIRST ENCOUNTERED DR. BOB ROTELLA, GOLFERS SPOKE OF psychologists in whispers, if they spoke about them at all.

In 1979, my first year at Furman University, one of my new classmates was a tennis player from Charlottesville, Virginia, named Frank Taylor. Frank had a book on athletic motivation, one of the first published works that made an effort to apply the science of psychology to sports. It was by two University of Virginia faculty members, Dr. Linda Bunker and Dr. Bob Rotella. I was intrigued. I read it and it helped me. I had a good career at Furman, becoming an All-American and a member of the Walker Cup team.

In 1983, I turned pro. On the PGA Tour in those days, players who talked to psychologists still didn't advertise the fact. But one day I played a practice round with Denis Watson. Denis, at the time, had risen suddenly out of the pack of Tour players to become one of the leading money winners. As we walked off the 18th green, I asked him what was behind his rapid improvement. He looked at me almost shyly. He confided that he had gone to see a sports psychologist in Virginia who had taught him better approaches to the mental side of the game.

"Bob Rotella?" I asked him.

Denis was startled that I knew the name. I told him I had read one of Rotella's books. I asked him about what Rotella had said that had helped him so much.

"Everything," Denis replied.

That was enough to persuade me to go to Charlottesville myself. Bob and I hit it off right away. We have been working together ever since, and Bob has become more than a consultant to me. He's become a friend and an important person in my life. Bob's ideas did not affect my game as suddenly or dramatically as they did Denis's. But they helped me, particularly in putting.

In seventeen years, Bob has never tried to change my putting stroke. To me, that makes sense. Golf has seen a tremendous variety of putting strokes and styles. If I close my eyes, I can see pictures of the great players putting—the crouching Nicklaus, the knock-kneed Palmer, the upright and flowing Crenshaw, and the determined and robotic Watson. They're all different. Tiger Woods, the best in the game right now, has a classic stroke. Tiger looks perfect standing over his putter. But there have also been greats such as Isao Aoki, Bobby Locke, and Billy Casper, with peculiar styles that few would dare emulate.

What Bob Rotella knows is that the secret to great putting is not in the stroke. It's in the mind. When you putt, your state of mind is more important than your mechanics.

Some people have a hard time understanding this. Because I am usually among the leaders in the Tour's putting statistics, I'm often asked if there's a secret to great putting. I usually reply that if there were a secret, I'd bottle it and sell it. I'd make a lot of money. I'd make a lot of golfers better putters and happier people.

But while there is no secret, there is a set of ideas—a way of thinking—that can help anyone become a better putter, perhaps even a great one. That's what you're going to find in this book. The good news is that these ideas make sense and they can be learned. I say this because I learned them and they became the foundation of my putting game. If I learned them, you can learn them, too. Maybe you've tried to improve your putting and haven't been successful. That doesn't mean you can't putt. It just means you've been going about it in the wrong way. The ability to putt well is inside you. You just have to get out of your own way and use it.

You're going to encounter concepts in these pages that may be new to you, concepts like trusting yourself, letting go, freeing it up, and loving the challenge of putting. You're going to learn how to develop a putting routine that works under pressure. You're going to find out what it feels like to love putting and to love making putts. You're going to learn some practice games and routines that I and other players use on the Tour. You're going to learn to understand the paradox that is at the heart of putting success: You make more putts when you don't care if you miss.

Judging by the way my pro-am partners generally act on the greens, these ideas may well be radically different from the thoughts you have now. A lot of the amateurs I see don't know how to trust themselves, don't know how to let go. They loathe and fear putting. They try very hard and they care desperately whether the ball goes in the hole. Not coincidentally, they don't putt very well.

If this sounds familiar to you, prepare for a change. If you can read, absorb, and adopt the ideas Bob Rotella teaches, you'll do more than sink a few putts. You'll enhance the pleasure you take from the game. You'll feel that a weight has been lifted from your shoulders.

Bob Rotella's ideas on putting are simple, but that doesn't mean they're easy to assimilate and follow. They may contradict attitudes you've carried around for most of your life. People often look at me in disbelief when I tell them I don't care that much if I miss a putt, that the result isn't as important to me as where my mind was when I stood over the ball. They don't understand what I've learned from Bob: If I can consistently achieve the right state of mind, I will consistently hole more putts.

Of course, if putting in the right frame of mind were easy,

everyone would do it. And then you wouldn't get the competitive advantage you're going to have when you finish this book.

For now, trust me. Bob Rotella is a master in his field. Thanks largely to him, golfers don't whisper about seeing psychologists any more. He has helped me improve as a player and as a putter. He can help you. Since you've got this book in your hands, I'm willing to venture two predictions. One is that you will never need another putting book. And the second is that you will enjoy reading this as much as you will enjoy putting in your next round of golf.

Foreword

....

by David Duval

ONE OF THE MOST CHALLENGING PUTTS I'VE EVER FACED WAS THE ONE I had on the final green of the 1999 Bob Hope Chrysler Classic. It wasn't the length or the break that made it hard, of course. The putt was only about seven feet, with a little tail at the end. If I'd had it on Thursday, I probably wouldn't have thought very much about it. But this wasn't Thursday. This was Sunday afternoon. It was an eagle putt to win the tournament. And it was for a score of 59, which would be the first sub-60 score anyone on the PGA Tour had ever shot in a final round. I knew that I might never have another chance to set that record. The circumstances surrounding the putt challenged my mind. And putting, I've learned, is all about your mind and your attitude.

Fortunately, I had something to fall back on under pressure, something I'd been taught by Bob Rotella—my putting routine. All that day, I'd been trying to do the same thing with every putt. For the first sixteen holes, it hadn't been so difficult. I'd started the day seven strokes behind the leader, Steve Pate. All I'd been thinking about was hitting the ball close to the flag and making birdie putts. I was hitting it well that day, and the putts I'd had generally weren't very long. It wasn't until I made birdie on the 16th hole to get to 11 under par for the day that I became fully aware of how low my score was. It was then that I realized what I had to do both to win and to shoot 59.

Once I started thinking about those things, the challenge got harder. When I hit my five-iron to the 18th green and saw it roll up close to the hole, it got harder still.

One of the principal elements of my routine is a decisive read. I don't want to second-guess myself. My caddie, Mitch Knox, and I didn't take a long time reading the putt. We both saw the same little break. I told myself to stick with my first instinct, not to waver, and to concentrate on executing my routine. One temptation in such a situation is to try to be too precise. Another is to focus too much on the outcome, on whether the putt falls. I resisted both. If you watched the tournament on TV and wondered what was going through my mind at that moment, here's the answer: I was telling myself not to think about the outcome and not to question what I was doing. I was thinking about preparation and routine. I wanted simply to hit the putt the way I'd hit the other putts that day, the way I'd practiced thousands of putts before.

I did, and it fell.

Some people, I suspect, might be a little disappointed to read this. They want to believe that there's some secret about putting that few players know and even fewer divulge, some act of self-hypnosis or mysticism that I used on that final green. I hear this when people ask me what I do with Bob Rotella. They think there must be something Doc and I discuss that he doesn't disclose in his books or his talks.

There isn't. Doc tells me the same things he'll tell you in this book. They're very simple. But great putters keep it simple.

I first met Bob Rotella when I was in college at Georgia Tech. My coach, Puggy Blackmon, invited him down each year to talk to the golf team. I remember that we worked that first time on routine, on attitude, and on confidence. Nearly a decade later, we're still working on the same things. Great putting isn't something you suddenly "get" and thereafter always have. It's a long-term challenge that you have to work on every day.

Doc didn't concern himself much with the mechanical aspects of my routine. As it happens, I have just a couple of physical keys I concentrate on when I practice. I try to keep my grip pressure light and consistent. I try to make sure the ball is positioned in the same place every time, just inside my left heel. Doc helped me realize that the particular mechanical elements I chose weren't as important as doing them consistently and believing in them.

We worked on ways to build confidence. As you'll read later on, Doc has some firm ideas about practice. He and I both believe that when you practice with a ball and a hole, it's vital to see the ball going into the hole. This means a heavy emphasis on practicing short putts. As a general rule, I spend a little time working on longer putts, to maintain my touch. But I spend hours at a time working on five-footers. As a result, I've become a really good putter from six or eight feet on into the hole. This benefits my whole game. I hit my longer putts more confidently, since I'm not worried about making the next one if I miss. I make birdies when I hit my chips and approach shots close.

We've worked longest on my attitude. This has been a gradual process with me. Some of it I've worked out by myself and some of it I've worked out with the help of Doc's advice. I'm still working on it. By way of an interim report, I can tell you that you must love putting if you want to be a great putter. You must always look forward to the challenge of holing the next putt. At the same time, you can't get wrapped up in putting statistics, or whether other people think you're a great putter, or how many putts fall. Even when you read them and stroke them perfectly, putts can miss for a lot of reasons, beginning with imperfect turf. So you have to set other standards for great putting—following your routine, observing your practice habits, maintaining your attitude. If you can honestly tell yourself that you're meeting those standards, then you're putting well.

I'd been a very good putter when I was a kid. But as I got bigger and was able to hit it longer, I focused more and more on the full swing. In high school and college, I'd characterize myself as a mediocre putter. That, of course, wasn't good enough to take me where I wanted to go in golf. You have to hit the ball well to win on the Tour. But there are a lot of players out there who hit it well. Week in, week out, the Tour becomes a putting contest. You're not going to have any success if you're not a great putter. There's no way around it.

To get from where I was when I turned pro to where I was when I shot 59 took a lot of thought, a lot of time, and a lot of work. Somewhere along the way, I had to shed a fear of failure when I putted. I can't tell you exactly when it happened. But gradually I found that I was coming to enjoy the moments when I walked onto a green and sized up a tough putt. Gradually, I learned to care less about whether that putt went in and more about whether I had done everything I could to give it a chance to go in.

I won't tell you that nowadays I have my mind exactly where it should be on every putt that I make. No golfer does. There are days when you hit it inside ten feet on each of the first six holes and don't make any of the putts. It's very easy to get down on yourself on such days. The difference now is that I can catch myself when my attitude wavers and get it back to where it should be sooner.

If you read this book carefully and absorb what it teaches, you can start to develop those abilities as well. You probably won't shoot 59. But sometime soon, late in a round that means something to you, you may find yourself sinking a putt your opponent was sure you'd miss. Flustered, he might even miss a putt that you thought he'd make. The match will turn. I can tell you from experience, there are few sweeter feelings to be had on a golf course.

The Heart of the Game

Putting—a game within a game—might justly be said to be the most important part of golf.

—BOBBY JONES

AS THE LAST TWOSOME APPROACHED THE 72ND GREEN OF THE 1998 Nissan Open, not many people in Los Angeles gave my friend and client Billy Mayfair much chance to win. Tiger Woods, playing a group ahead of Billy, had just birdied the final hole to take a one-stroke lead. Tiger was charging. He had birdied three of the last four holes.

The Nissan Open that year was played at Valencia Country Club, and the 18th hole was a long par-5. Billy had not birdied it all week and he did not reach it in two strokes on this occasion. He hit his three-wood into a bunker to the right of the green. But Billy then hit a nice explosion shot to about five feet. He made that putt to force a play-off.

Even then, it was all but assumed that Tiger would win the play-off, which began on the same par-5. Tiger hits the ball much longer than Billy, whose length off the tee is about average for the PGA Tour. Even those who understood that good putting is much more important than length off the tee found reason to favor Tiger: Billy Mayfair has a very unorthodox putting stroke, the kind of stroke that television commentators love to criticize, love to say won't hold up under pressure.

That putting stroke was what initially brought Billy and me together.

Billy grew up in Phoenix. From the time he started playing golf, he enjoyed putting. He had little choice. His parents weren't wealthy and when they dropped him off at a municipal golf course called Papago Park, they couldn't give him money for greens fees or range balls. The only thing a kid could do for free at Papago Park was putt and chip around the big, crowned practice green.

So Billy did, five days a week after school. He developed into a very good putter. Even though he never hit the ball enormous distances, he won a lot of junior tournaments. He won the U.S. Public Links. He won the U.S. Amateur.

He did all of this with the idiosyncratic putting stroke he'd developed at Papago Park. Billy did not take the putter straight back and bring it straight through the ball. He drew the club back outside the target line—the line he intended for the ball to travel as it left the putter blade. As he started his forward stroke, it looked as if he would pull every putt to his left. But at the last instant, Billy straightened his blade until it was perpendicular to the target line. And he made a lot of putts that way, even though the purists who saw him insisted he was cutting the ball, coming across it from right to left.

Billy, of course, didn't grow up knowing many purists at Papago Park. All he knew was that he had a putting stroke that got the ball in the hole. He assumed it was a stroke that went straight up and down the line of the putt. Why wouldn't he?

When Billy got out on the Tour in 1989, he did quite well. He made enough money to keep his playing card in 1989 and moved up to twelfth on the money list in 1990. But then he started to slip. He developed problems with his short game, especially his putting.

One reason, Billy now thinks, is the way Tour courses are equipped. Every one of them has a big practice range with grass tees. On every practice range there is an unlimited supply of fresh golf balls—real ones, not range balls. For a kid from Papago Park who could never afford to hit all the balls he wanted, this was all but irresistible. Billy started to spend more of his practice time working on his full swing.

At the same time, he started to listen to the critics of his putting stroke. There were so many of them he decided they had to be right, and he set about trying to give himself a classic putting stroke, straight back and straight through. This was what he thought he needed to break into the ranks of tournament winners.

A player who starts spending too much time on his full swing and not enough on his wedges and chips will soon find himself facing longer putts for par. Even the best players hit, on average, only thirteen or so greens per round. Five times a round, they have to get up and down, and if their short game isn't sharp they're going to be looking at a lot of six- and seven-foot putts they feel they have to make.

If they do this at the same time they're thinking about changing their putting stroke, thinking about taking the blade straight back and forth, they will soon find themselves in trouble. If you're obsessed with some model of the perfect stroke, the first time you miss a putt you think you should have made, you're going to start having doubts about your stroke. Pretty soon, you'll be riven with doubt, as self-conscious as a teenager wearing a new outfit he thinks the others kids deem ugly. And you'll be just as awkward.

In fact, when Billy first came to see me in 1991, he told me he had developed a case of the yips. His scores were going up. He was in danger of losing his card.

What he had, I thought, was not the yips. It was a case of misplaced priorities and a way of thinking that wasn't working on the putting green. I suggested that Billy stop trying to fix his putting stroke. It had never been broken. In trying to fix it, he'd lost his focus on the true business at hand on the green, which is rolling the ball into the hole. I told him I didn't care whether he cut the ball when he putted. I didn't care whether he stroked his putts standing on his head. I just wanted him to think about his target and let the putt go. I wanted him to rediscover the practice priorities he'd had as a kid and spend more time working on his wedges and his chipping.

Billy did. He went on to win his first Tour event in 1993 and to build a solid career for himself. He won the Tour Championship in 1995 at Southern Hills on some of the fastest greens in the country.

All of that history was on my mind as I watched that Nissan Open play-off begin. I think it was on Billy's, too.

"I knew Tiger would have an advantage on a par-five," he told me later. "But then he drove into the rough and I knew he wasn't going to be able to reach it in two. That meant the hole was probably going to be decided with wedge shots and putts. I thought to myself, 'Okay, Tiger. The game's on my court now.'"

Billy Mayfair reaffirmed, in that moment, his knowledge of one of the abiding truths about putting. The challenge of making a putt to win, to set a personal record, is what golf is all about. That's why professional golfers practice putting as much as they do—because they want to savor the joy of meeting that challenge. The best and smartest of them realize something else as well. Putting is fun.

Billy drove into the fairway and hit his second shot about eighty-five yards from the green. Tiger couldn't reach the green from the rough. He left his second thirty yards away.

Billy's wedge was lovely to watch. It hit about eight feet behind the hole and spun back, coming to rest about six feet away. Tiger hit his pitch past the hole and left himself a fifteen-foot birdie putt.

Tiger's putt was a good one, but it slid past the hole. He sank to his knees, chagrined.

Billy used the time he had while Tiger went through his putting routine. He walked around his putt, checked out everything he could see. But he had known from the time he stepped onto the green what this putt was going to do. It was not quite on the same line as the putt he'd made on the 72nd hole, but it was close. It would be uphill. It would be straight.

"When you're putting really well," he told me later, "you see a line. It's like a baseball player who's hitting really good and says the ball looks like it's barely moving. Your vision is different. I saw my line, just right of dead straight. Uphill. I had a pretty good idea in the back of my mind how hard to hit it."

Billy had the wisdom, as he paced about and continued to inspect the green, not to let anything change this solid first impression. Instead, his observation only strengthened his initial read.

Then it was his turn. There were a lot of things he could have thought about. He could have thought about the fact that he had last won a tournament three seasons before. He could have thought about how impressive Tiger had been ten months previously in winning the Masters by twelve strokes. He could have thought about what would happen on the next hole if he missed his putt. He could have thought about the statistics that show that Tour players make only about half of their six-footers. He could have thought about his nerves.

Fortunately, he didn't. Billy was experienced. He knew that

the nerves that accompany a PGA Tour play-off were not something to fear. They were something to welcome. He knew that all the hours of practice had been spent precisely to help him get to a spot where his nerves would jangle.

"All I really thought about," he told me later, "was making sure that I did my routine and saw my target well. I let the putt go."

His target was just a bit to the right of the center of the hole. When he's putting well, Billy tells me, he seems to see everything in slow motion. The ball leaves the putter blade and rolls like a big, heavy beach ball. It is as if he can see every revolution it makes, watch it bump gently over each blade of grass.

This time, everything went slowly. The ball rolled ponderously but inexorably. It was dead straight. He knew from the instant he struck it that his touch had been good. It was a nice, firm hit. He watched the ball cover the target point he'd chosen and fall into the cup. An instant later, pandemonium erupted and Billy felt a deep sense of satisfaction.

"You don't get too many chances to beat Tiger," he told me. "And when you do have a chance, you want to take it."

I love the way Billy handled the situation. He wanted to beat Tiger Woods. But he was able to discipline his thinking enough to shove that thought out of his field of focus, along with all other distracting ideas. He thought only of seeing the target he wanted and letting the putt roll. That was why he made the putt.

• • •

I RECOUNT THIS story not solely because I enjoy looking back on a triumphant moment for a nice guy who works hard at his game and deserves everything he gets—though I do.

I recount it because it shows so much about the subject of this book—loving putting, enjoying putting, making putts, making putts that matter, making putts to win. In the pages that follow, I'm going to use Billy's story, and the stories of many other golfers, on and off the professional tours, to tell you how to become a good putter, even a great putter.

I offer this assurance to you: If you can absorb the principles in this book and put them into practice the way Billy Mayfair did, you are going to become a much better putter than most of the people around you, unless, by chance, the people around you are the other members of the Ryder Cup team. You're never going to putt worse than decently. And on your good days, you will putt very well indeed.

Most golf instruction books pay scant attention to putting. They start with the fundamentals of the full swing. They add putting as an afterthought. Some of the classics of instructional literature don't even address putting.

I never thought about golf that way, in part because I came to golf after years spent in other sports. As a kid and a college student, I played basketball and lacrosse. As the director of sports psychology at the University of Virginia, I coached athletes in the gamut of intercollegiate sports. Twenty years ago, when golfers started coming to me and asking for help with their game, I was able to look at golf with relatively fresh eyes.

I knew that in any sport, there were fundamental skills that good coaches emphasized in their teaching and insisted their players execute. In basketball, for instance, I knew that every great team had a good attitude, rebounded well, played defense well, and shot free throws well. Those skills separated them from the merely good teams and the less-than-good ones. A merely good team wins on nights when its shooters are hot. Great teams win on nights when they don't shoot well, because they always play defense, rebound, and shoot free throws. And they always take the floor with a good attitude.

When I started studying golfers, it became immediately apparent to me that good putting was the functional equivalent of good defense, good rebounding, and good shooting from the foul line. I noticed that even the great players didn't bring their best swings to the course more than half the time. But the great ones almost always found ways to turn in a low score anyway. They did it with their short game and their putting. When I started working with golfers, I insisted that they spend a lot of time developing imagination and touch with their scoring clubs, their wedges and putters. At the time, this was not a fashionable view among golf instructors. Most instructors had spent their lives trying to figure out the full swing. They were in love with the mechanics of the driver and the seven-iron. That's what they wanted to teach, and that's what they encouraged their pupils to practice.

That emphasis has shifted in the past two decades, though not necessarily because of my influence. It's the simple logic of the game. No matter how skilled you are with the long clubs, you're going to make roughly 40 percent of your shots with your putter. Moreover, on the PGA and LPGA tours, it's very difficult to separate yourself from the pack by improving your ball striking. Everybody out there can hit the ball well when he or she is on. The putting game is the place to look if you want to get a competitive advantage, to shave the stroke or so per round that makes the difference between making cuts and missing cuts, between winning tournaments and not winning them.

The rule applies no matter what type of golf you play. If you're an average male player who keeps a handicap, you generally shoot in the high 80s or low 90s. Once in a while you make a routine par, hitting your driver into the fairway, your iron onto the green, and getting down in two putts. Far more often, you're around the green in regulation figures, but you're not on it. To make par, you need to wedge the ball onto the green and make a putt. Most often, you don't do that. You probably three-putt more often than you get up and down. But if you putted well, your scores would drop.

In fact, good players know that putting accounts for even more of their success or failure than the strokes on the scorecard would indicate. Seve Ballesteros once explained that on days when he felt that his putting was on, when he could count on getting the ball into the hole when he had to, his whole game changed. Off the tee and on his approach shots, good putting gave him a cocky, go-for-broke attitude that was essential to the production of his best shots. He could afford to be cocky because he knew his putter would rescue him when he made a mistake. Conversely, when Seve felt his putting was off, his whole game suffered. He got tight and careful with his long clubs. He started trying to steer the ball. His good shots turned mediocre and his bad shots turned disastrous.

Good putting helps your golf game the way a strong foundation works for a house. If you putt well, it's easier to hit your wedges and chips. If you can hit your wedges and chips, you'll hit your irons more freely. And if you're confident about your irons, it will help your tee shots.

I like to see players not only accept the importance of putting but revel in it. The ideal golfing temperament would instinctively love putting. A golfer with this ideal temperament would feel a quiet surge of joy every time he stepped onto a putting green. He would think, Oh, good! Now we get to putt! This is where I come to life, this is where I can express my imagination and artistry, this is where I can kick some butt!

Very few people manage to maintain that sort of attitude throughout their golfing careers. A lot of kids seem to have it. But there are socialization pressures at work in golf that want them to become cautious, careful, and eventually fearful about their putting. Over the many years of a golfer's life, it's easy to succumb.

All too many players feel a sense of dread as they walk toward a green, much as they might if they were walking into a dentist's office. They think that nothing good can happen to them there. If they've reached the green in regulation figures, they worry about three-putting and wasting the good shots that got them there. If they have a good birdie chance, they worry about blowing it. If they've struggled just to reach the green, big numbers float through their brains.

If you wonder whether this describes you, let me ask a clarifying question. How often do you look at a couple of three-foot putts and find yourself saying to your opponent, "Good-good?"

This kind of thinking can afflict even the greatest of players. Ben Hogan was one example. When he was winning tournaments, Hogan wrote and spoke of putting with equanimity, as an integral part of the game that could be handled with the right measures of practice, concentration, and relaxation. But as he got older, and his ball striking became virtually flawless, Hogan's attitude toward putting changed. He began to see it as an injustice that putting counted for so much in tournament golf. He began to loathe putting. Once, late in his career, Hogan played a pretournament practice round with the young Billy Casper, who was one of the best putters of all time. During the round, Hogan played his usual immaculate shots from tee to green. He made nearly no putts that mattered. Casper, meanwhile, was all over the golf course with his long shots. But he putted brilliantly. When the round was over, Casper had something like a 66 and Hogan something like 71. Hogan owed Casper some money. As he paid off his lost bet, Hogan sourly told Casper, "If you couldn't putt, you'd be selling hot dogs behind the tenth green."

Hogan, perhaps, thought he was putting Casper in his place,

thought he was making the point that he had a much better golf swing than Casper. What he was really saying was, "I can't play this game anymore." Any golfer whose improved ball striking becomes an excuse for hating to putt is in danger of wasting all the time he's devoted to his full swing.

I see this syndrome threatening many of the successful professionals I work with. Typically, they made it to the PGA or LPGA Tour by first learning how to get the ball in the hole. Many of them, like Billy Mayfair, spent much of their childhood hanging around a putting green. Dottie Pepper tells me that when she was a girl, she'd get on her bike on summer mornings just after dawn. She'd go to a golf course near her home called McGregor Links and go out to the 16th green. She knew that the first players wouldn't tee off till the sun had been up for an hour or so. They wouldn't reach the 16th for several hours after that. That gave her lots of time, and she used it to chip, putt, play sand shots, and putt some more. When the first golfers reached the 16th tee, she raked the traps and took off, only to return hours later for more putting in the twilight.

Quite often, as Billy Mayfair did, this kind of player finds that his arrival on the Tour is a great opportunity to work on his full swing, perhaps the best such opportunity he's ever had. He no longer has to devote time to school. There are no restrictions on how many range balls he can hit. He has access to the best swing teachers in the world. Quite commonly, these players become better, more consistent ball strikers at thirty than they were at twenty-two.

But this only puts more pressure on their putting. They can't help noticing that just as much as it did when they were juniors, putting determines success in professional tournaments. Most of them boil down to putting contests. They realize that putting is almost the only culprit keeping them from the success they've dreamed of since they were kids. This can poison their attitude toward putting, turning them from a kid who naturally putted well into a middle-aged man, like Ben Hogan became, who makes sour remarks about someone else's putting success.

My job, with the players I work with personally, as well as with the readers of this book, is to make sure that doesn't happen. It's to help you develop a great putting mind if you've never had one and to help you preserve it if you grew up being a fine putter. It's to help you embark on a lifelong love affair with putting. With such a mind, you can become an excellent putter.

Without it, you might as well stay on the practice range, because your real game is hitting balls. It isn't playing golf. Golf is a game of scoring. If you want to score, you must putt. If you want to score well, you must putt well. It's as simple as that.

Let me assure you, this isn't impossible. All athletic skills have mental and physical components. Some events—the uneven parallel bars, for instance—require highly developed physical skills. Putting isn't a complicated physical skill. Compared to the uneven parallel bars, it's a snap. If you can walk and roll a ball with your hands, or throw it underhand to a partner, you can handle the physical challenge of putting. Putting is primarily a mental challenge, and the mental side of putting requires some effort, some thought, and some discipline. But if you're reading this book, you have all the tools you need. You can do what so many of the greats of the game have done. You can build your game from the green back toward the tee and have the sweet satisfaction of seeing your scores drop as a result. Or you can continue to fear and dread putting.

The choice is yours.

The Putter Jack Nicklaus
Sees in the Mirror

> *You have to feel that you are a great putter to be one. If you start to tell yourself that you can't putt, you can bet your bottom peso that you won't be able to get it in the hole from three feet.*
>
> —LEE TREVINO

A FEW YEARS AGO, I WAS INVITED TO SPEAK AT A FUND-RAISING DIN-ner for the golf program at Georgia Tech. Jack Nicklaus, whose son Michael was then attending Tech, was the featured speaker. I was, of course, eager to hear anything he had to say about golf and the way he played it.

One remark Jack made struck both me and the members of the audience. He was speaking about facing a crucial putt on the last hole of a tournament.

"I have never three-putted the last hole of a tournament or missed from inside five feet on the last hole of a tournament," Jack said. He continued with his talk.

That was more than one member of the audience, a man in

his sixties, was able to bear. When question time came, he stood up.

"Uh, Mr. Nicklaus," he said, "I really enjoyed your talk. But the statement you made about never three-putting the last green of a tournament or never missing from inside five feet on the last hole of a tournament—well, I was watching you in the Senior PGA just last month and I distinctly remember you missed a three-footer on the last hole."

"Sir, you're wrong," Jack said firmly. "I have never three-putted the last hole of a tournament or missed inside five feet on the last hole of a tournament."

"But, Mr. Nicklaus," the man objected. "I have it on tape. I could send it to you. Lee Trevino was in the broadcast booth and he said you never used to miss short putts but now you miss them to the right sometimes and then you missed an entire cup to the right—"

"There's no need to send me anything, sir," Jack interrupted him. "I was there. I have never three-putted the last green of a tournament or missed from inside five feet on the last green of a tournament."

Jack finished his talk and headed for the airport where his jet was parked. He has a busy schedule.

But the questioning man lingered, and he approached me. "Dr. Rotella," he said, "what's wrong with Nicklaus? Why can't he just admit it? You're the psychology expert. Can you explain it?"

I asked the man whether he played golf.

"Yes," he said.

"What's your handicap?" I asked.

"About sixteen," he said.

"And if you missed a short putt on the last hole of a tournament, you'd remember it and admit it," I observed.

"Of course," he confirmed.

"So let me get this straight," I said. "You're a sixteen handicap, and Jack Nicklaus is the greatest golfer ever, and you want Jack to think like you?"

The man had no answer.

THE POINT OF the story, of course, is not whether Jack Nicklaus has ever missed a short putt on the last hole of a tournament. Of course he has. The point is that Jack's memory works differently from the memories of a lot of golfers.

We are raised in a culture of red marks. When kids take math tests, their papers come back with a red **x** next to the problems they answered incorrectly. The child is taught to review his mistake carefully, to remember it, and not to make it again. And so it goes through life. Quite naturally, therefore, we are people who tend to dwell on our mistakes. We remember them. We replay them in our minds. Once in a while, in some endeavors, I suppose this does some good. If you paint houses for a living, and you climb to the top of your scaffold and discover you've forgotten your paintbrushes, it's probably not a bad thing to remember your carelessness and remind yourself forever after to bring your brushes.

But in putting, as Mark Twain once observed in another context, the inability to forget is infinitely more devastating than the inability to remember. In that sense, Jack Nicklaus was indeed a talented putter. He had selective amnesia. He was able to block from his mind all the missed putts. He kept and replayed the memories of made putts. He was able to retain a firm belief that the next one was going in the hole. He was able to think of himself as a great putter.

Because he thought that way, he was able to *be* a great putter. As William James, the pioneering American psychologist, shrewdly stated in the nineteenth century, people tend to become what they think about themselves. This simple truth is the basis for much of what I do as a sports psychologist.

It also points to the first step in any serious program to make yourself a better putter. You must examine yourself and your attitude toward putting. You have to assess your self-image regarding putting.

Are you the sort of player who gripes and complains all the time about his putting? When you step onto a green, are you glum and fearful, expecting the worst? Do you silently pray that your opponents will concede your next putt? Have you decided that you simply were born without putting talent, and this will be your burden to bear till the end of your golfing days?

If so, you need a new attitude. And the first step in getting a new attitude about putting is to change the way your memory works.

When I suggest this to players, I often hear this objection. "Whoa, Doc. I didn't wake up one morning and decide I was a bad putter just for the heck of it. I'm a realist. I think I'm a bad putter because I've missed a lot of putts! I can't just decide I'm a good putter when I know I'm not."

First of all, it's foolish to evaluate your putting if your mind has been holding you back. You may well have missed some putts in the past. But if you attempted them with a mind full of doubt, if you tried to steer the ball rather than let the stroke happen naturally—in short, if you putted with the wrong attitude—then those misses aren't relevant to the caliber of putter you can be. What would you think of a football coach who told you you weren't fast enough to play if your time trial occurred when you had a sprained ankle? You'd think he was unfair. Yet people routinely decide they're bad putters on the basis of putts they've missed when they've been carrying around a handicap far more damaging than a sprained ankle.

Second, many people use "realism" as an excuse for negative thinking. Jack Nicklaus has undoubtedly missed more putts than your entire Saturday foursome combined. But Jack either chooses not to remember the putts he's missed or he's blessed with a natural tendency to forget them. Jack remembers instead the putts he's made, the putts that will help him be confident the next time he has a critical ten-footer.

In that he's like many other great athletes. Michael Jordan used to say that he never pondered the mistakes he'd made in a basketball game for more than ten or fifteen minutes after the game was over. In that time, he analyzed what went wrong and learned whatever he could learn from it. Then he focused his mind on getting ready for the next game. Other players hung their heads for hours and berated themselves for mistakes. Jordan saw that they were destroying themselves. He never did that.

It's not easy to discipline your mind the way Michael Jordan and Jack Nicklaus did. But the fact that it isn't easy doesn't mean it's impossible. It means that there's something you can do through strength of mind that will separate you from the vast majority of your competitors, just as it did for Nicklaus and Jordan.

There's nothing worse for your putting than dwelling on the putts you've missed. In fact, it's like multiplying the effects of a missed putt. If you lie awake after a bad round, replaying missed putts in your brain, it's psychologically no different from actually going out on a green and missing them again, over and over. You're training yourself to believe that you can't putt.

But, in truth (or reality, if that's a term you prefer) if you've played golf any length of time, you've made a lot of putts. You could remember those putts. How about that twelve-footer that saved par the last time you played? Or the four-footer that you had to make to win a Nassau against your buddies? Or that curling, twenty-foot birdie putt you sank a week ago? Why not remember those?

You can if you choose to. Training the memory is possible. Try this. The next few times you play, make a conscious effort not to add up the three-putts you made or dwell on the five-footer that lipped out. Forget them. They're gone. Instead, pick the best three putts you made in that round. Think about them. The next morning, when you wake up, remember them. Relive them.

If you do that after every round you'll be on your way to developing at least one important part of your golf game into the equal of Jack Nicklaus's.

CHANGING THE WAY you remember is half the battle in changing the way you perceive yourself as a putter. And changing your self-perception is half the battle in developing from a mediocre putter to a great one.

I am constantly amazed at how frequently golfers cripple themselves with poor self-perceptions. They decide that great putters are born, not made. They decide they lost in the genetic lottery. They have no talent, no ability to putt well. From there, it's a short step to thinking that there's not really much point in trying to improve, because they're never going to be good putters. They're comfortable with the way they've always thought on the greens. It hasn't worked for them, of course, but they're used to it, and changing would require effort and effort wouldn't pay off anyway. They take a perverse pride in describing themselves as bad putters. They sit in the grill after their rounds, their wallets lighter, and grouse about how they couldn't buy a putt, can't ever make a putt. They rehash all the putts they've missed, as if to corroborate the thesis that when it comes to putting, they have neither skill nor luck—except for bad luck.

They embody the self-fulfilling prophecy. They persuade themselves that they have no talent at putting, no skill, no luck. And then when they actually putt, their brains naturally assume they have no chance to make it. It's true that they have no chance—no chance to get into the relaxed, confident state of mind that is conducive to good putting.

It's my job to convince such people that even if they haven't had much success in the past with their putting, their perception of themselves should be governed not by what they've done, but by what they'd like to do. But getting this idea across is not easy.

For one thing, many golfers find poor putting to be a convenient rationale for failing to play well. It gives them a tolerable excuse. These are the sorts of people who claim that they hit the ball very well, but they never win, or even play to their potential, because they can't putt. Implicit in what they say is the notion that ball striking is real golf, and putting is a sissy add-on, and if they're not good at the sissy add-on part, well, hey, can Jean-Claude Van Damme do the tango?

They remind me of a guy who grows a scraggly, miserable-looking, unattractive goatee. Then he uses the goatee to explain his inability to get women to go out with him. He'd have dates, he implies, but not many women are hip enough to appreciate his manly growth. In truth, of course, he's afraid that women will reject him even if he looks his best. He maintains the goatee to protect himself from that disconcerting prospect. In much the same way, people can find it useful to cultivate a perception that they are lousy putters.

On the other hand, consider the player who believes he's a great putter. He thinks back pleasantly to the good putts he's made. He never gripes, he never moans. He never lets himself be thrown by something like a bumpy green. When people ask how he's putting, he usually responds, "Great!" If he didn't make a lot of putts in his last round, he'll say, "Great. I feel like I'm due to hole a bunch of them."

Because of such players' self-perception, it's easier for them to stay in practice. They *like* going out on the practice green. It gives them a little chance to show off. It's the same syndrome that explains why people in the best physical condition are the ones most likely to be found in gyms. It's because they like the shape they're in and they like the chance to show off what their bodies can do.

These players tend to be able to monitor their own attitudes the same way an athlete monitors his weight. They catch themselves whenever they find their attitudes souring. They make the necessary adjustment when they're only a little bit off. They have a much easier time getting and staying confident than the player who periodically throws a pity party for himself and wallows in his own bile.

Because of their self-perception, players with good attitudes find it much easier to putt in competition. They don't step up to a long first putt thinking fearfully of a possible three-putt. They step up to a long putt calmly and confidently. When they have a testy little five-footer for par, they don't feel obliged to give themselves a putting seminar before they stroke the ball, in the process tightening their muscles and spoiling their rhythm. They're more likely to step up to the ball, go through their putting routine, and stroke it gracefully and accurately.

Because of their self-perception, they are immune to doubts and fears about their technique. In fact, they tend to think the rest of the world should copy them.

When I was a kid, the greatest putter in the world was probably Bobby Locke, of South Africa. Locke married a woman from my hometown, Rutland, Vermont. In the summers, I'd see him once in a while at the Rutland Country Club, where I caddied. Sometimes I carried his bag or shagged balls for him.

Locke had a very unorthodox, highly personal putting stroke. On his backswing, he flexed his wrists and hooded the face of his putter in a way that you would never see on the Tour today. He liked to think that he could spin the ball different ways for different putts, "hooking" right-to-left putts and "slicing" those that broke the other way. Despite all that, Bobby Locke could putt.

Locke, of course, didn't think his putting style was unorthodox. He thought his putting style was eminently logical and reasonable. He figured it was the rest of the world that had a problem. In that way, he reminds me of Billy Mayfair when Billy is thinking well about his putting.

That's the way good putters see themselves. That's why they're good putters.

I'm not trying to suggest that changing your putting self-image is easy. It's not. It can be difficult. But improving at golf is not supposed to be easy. If it were, golf wouldn't be the game it is. Welcome the fact that it's hard and that most people won't do it. If you need an incentive, consider this: Thinking the way you have always thought will almost certainly assure that you putt the way you have always putted.

Try this bit of mental practice. Spend fifteen minutes each night thinking of nothing but making putts. Relive putts you've made and savor the sight and the feeling again. Think about putts you might have in your next round of golf. See them going in the hole.

As with any visualization exercise, this one won't help you if you don't apply yourself to it wholeheartedly. Try to imagine as richly and precisely as you can how the grass felt under your feet, how the hole looked, how the ball rolled, how it sounded as it plunked into the cup. Remember the way your eyes and brain interacted, the way your body felt as you stroked the putt. If you can do it, fifteen minutes of this is worth as much as or more than the same amount of time practicing actual putts, particularly if you've mastered the physical fundamentals.

Change the way you converse about putting. Banish any gripes and complaints from your vocabulary. Change the subject if someone in the group wants to moan about putting. If someone asks you about your putting, say it's fine. Tell him about a putt you've made or tell him you expect to break out with a bunch of birdie putts any day.

Some people tell me that they're just not comfortable being Little Orphan Annie about their putting. Visualization exercises are a little too touchy-feely for them. They'd rather not talk optimistically about their putting because they think it's boastful, or they're afraid their opponents might mock them if they later miss a putt. Well, you can't be successful at putting if you're letting fear of missed putts dictate your behavior. But if you're the quiet, modest type who was taught not to boast, that's all right. The only rule is that you not entertain negative ideas about your putting. You can cultivate a laconic shrug of the shoulders for use when the conversation turns to your putting, or putting in general.

But on the green, where it counts, make sure you're thinking like Jack Nicklaus and Bobby Locke.

How Good Putters Think

*On every putt, see the ball going into the hole
with your mind's eye.*

—GARY PLAYER

GOLFERS GENERALLY DON'T BECOME MY CLIENTS WHEN THEY'RE PLAYing the best golf of their careers. They come to me when they have problems with their games. Hal Sutton was no exception.

Hal had once been touted as the successor to Jack Nicklaus. He won early in his professional career and, it seemed, easily. At the age of twenty-five, he led the Tour in earnings and captured a major championship, the PGA. But after a time the victories stopped, for many reasons. One of those reasons was putting.

Hal was the sort of player who could hit the ball very accurately. He was usually near the top of the Tour statistics in hitting greens in regulation. But once he got on the green, his thoughts tended to be less clear, less certain than they were on the tee or in the fairway. If he was fifteen feet away, he told me he felt as if he had one side of his brain telling him to make the putt, while the other was saying, "Don't waste that good drive and good iron shot by three-putting." He'd start to feel the anguish of the three-putt before he'd even hit his first putt. So, of course, his first putts were sometimes timid and cautious. Or, if he'd been timid and cautious on the previous hole, he could be much too bold. When we started working together, Hal already realized he had to get rid of that negative, doubting voice that he was hearing.

As I do with most players, I tried to impress Hal with the importance of a routine for both long shots and putts, a routine that emphasized looking at the target and letting it go—that is, making the stroke freely and confidently. Hal intuitively grasped what I was telling him when it came to long shots. He hunts as a hobby. He could relate what I was telling him to hunting. When he hunted, he saw a target and, without thinking much about it, aimed his gun and fired. That image helped him develop a free, confident routine on the tee and in the fairway.

On the green, it was harder. One day I asked him to try a little experiment. We were in Charlottesville and we went over to the golf course at Keswick Hall, a resort outside of town. I asked Hal to play a round with me using his normal routine for long shots. But on the greens, I wanted him to putt with his eyes not on the ball but on the target.

Hal was skeptical, but he agreed. He tried it on the practice green for half an hour. Then he putted the entire round with this altered routine. Normally, he would line himself and his club up, look at the ball, look at the target, look at the ball again, and stroke the putt. This time, he used the same routine, but instead of returning his eyes to the ball after his look at the target, he kept his gaze fixed on where he wanted the ball to go. He stroked the putt seeing the target, not the ball.

The result is framed and hangs in the grill at Keswick Hall. It's a scorecard showing that Hal set the course record that day with a 63.

Now, I'm not suggesting that anyone can set a course record if he putts with his eyes on the target instead of the ball. Hal never used this method in a tournament. It was an exercise to help him understand the feeling of being focused on the target just as much when he putted as he was when he hit longer shots. I think it's a useful experiment for any golfer to try and I often encourage players I work with to do it. I think it would be very interesting to see what would happen if a group of them gave it a real test in competition. They don't, primarily because they're skittish about the possibility of mishitting or actually whiffing a putt.

The exercise is helpful to a lot of players because it drama- tizes the way good putters think. It's a little bit like taking a child's head between your hands and directing his gaze pre- cisely where you want him to look. In this case, it focuses the golfer's attention where it should be—the target.

* * *

Let's suppose, for a moment, that someone had invented a device that could read minds. You could aim this device at anyone's head, and a computer would print out what the individual was thinking.

Here's what you might see if you aimed this device at the head of someone who sees himself as a poor putter.

My putter blade is a little off line, let's adjust it. . . . If I miss this I'll probably lose the hole. . . . I've already three-putted twice today, don't want to do that again. . . . Dammit, it's only four feet, I SHOULD make it. . . . Of course, last Saturday I blew a three-footer . . . hmm, the ground under my feet feels like it's got a little bit of slope to it . . . could it really be a straight putt? . . . No, God wouldn't give me a straight putt . . . maybe better play it to break bit left. . . . Why am I always the one who has these four-footers to make and why am I always the one who winds up having to pay for the drinks after the round. . . . Is that a pitch mark I see in my line? This club's gotta get a new superintendent. . . . Wonder if I should hit driver on the next tee or go with the three-wood? This one's gonna be fast, it's downhill . . . don't want to roll it too far past if I miss it . . . all right, now concentrate! Make sure you take the club back straight, perfect stroke now, keep your head still, don't peek. . . .

Here's what you might see if you aimed at the head of a good putter facing the same spot.

My target is that little tuft of raised grass on the lip of the cup.

And that's all you'd see.

A lot of people, at this point, would look at this putative computer screen and object. "Wait a minute," they'd say. "That's all he's thinking? What is he, thick?"

No, the good putter is not thick. But he has a mind so quiet and so clear that it might strike many people as a bit obtuse. In our society, we're been educated to revere thought, to revere the conscious mind. And in some endeavors, that's fine. If you're designing the airplane I'm going to fly in next week, for instance, I want you to be very conscious and to think through everything in detail.

But this cultural pressure makes it difficult for some people to clear their minds. I used to ask students to work on this by spending a short period of time trying to focus their minds on something small and simple, like the top of a ballpoint pen. Look at it, think about its function. But think of nothing else for five minutes or ten minutes, or fifteen minutes. You might want to try this exercise. If you can clear your mind to focus only on the tip of the pen, you can clear it to focus on the target or line when you're putting.

In putting, you want to narrow the focus of your thoughts as much as possible, to shut down a lot of the conscious, thinking parts of the brain, the parts that give instructions. Putting is one of those physical tasks that are best left to the less intellectual, less rational parts of the mind. You don't, for instance, start jogging and consciously think, Better increase my respiration, take more breaths per second to increase my oxygen intake. A subconscious part of your brain takes care of your breathing for you. If you're driving along on a highway and you're talking to someone in the seat next to you, you're easily able to continue the conversation while you pull into the passing lane and overtake a truck. A subconscious part of your brain smoothly handles the driving, allowing you to continue your conversation. In fact, you probably drive more smoothly this way than you would if you stopped talking and paid careful attention to your driving. You certainly drive more smoothly this way than you could when you were just sixteen, driving on a highway for the first time, and carefully using your conscious brain to control every movement.

If you're putting, you'll make your best stroke and hole the most putts if you think only of your target. You won't sink all your putts, of course. Not even putting machines can do that. But you'll sink more putts thinking this way than you will any other way.

I don't know precisely why our bodies work this way. They simply do. I see evidence of it quite frequently. Little kids are often great putters because they simply pick up a putter and roll the ball at the hole. They don't know enough to think their way through the stroke, reminding themselves of all the tips they've had and the lessons they've taken. They just roll it. Older golfers sometimes dramatically improve their putting when they reach a stage in life when they don't worry so much about scores or competitions, or anything else for that matter. They just like seeing the ball roll into the hole.

Some folks understand this intuitively because they haven't been exposed to a lot of the theories and ideas and old wives' tales that abound about putting. Some years ago, shortly after I started counseling golfers, I visited my parents, who were just taking up golf. My mother, Laura, asked curiously what it was that I was telling golfers that they found so helpful they paid me for it.

"A lot of it's about putting, Mom," I said. "I help them to think about the target when they're putting."

"Well, for heaven's sake," she said. "What else would they think about?"

"Mom," I told her, "you'd be amazed."

And she would. Even professional golfers are prone to undermine their own putting with thoughts about their stroke, or making the cut, or keeping their card, or not three-putting. I see this fairly often with Tour pros who let their minds wander from the target for the first thirty holes of a tournament. By that time, they're three or four over par and they figure they're not going to make the cut. So they stop being careful, stop being conscious, start thinking only about their targets, and hole a few birdie putts coming in. Sometimes they make enough putts to survive the cut. Then they go back to undermining themselves on Saturday.

They don't mean to undermine themselves, of course. Some of them don't know that dwelling on the results of putts rather than on the simple act of rolling the ball to a target doesn't help them. They don't know that constantly being aware of the score doesn't help them. Or, if they know these things, they haven't developed the mental discipline to shut those thoughts out of their minds when they putt. They might think that if they lose track of the score and don't worry much about whether the ball goes in the hole, they're not trying hard enough, not giving 100 percent. And how can they compete with Tiger Woods if they're not giving 100 percent?

But it's pretty certain Tiger isn't thinking that way. In the clutch, at least, Tiger is thinking of the target. That's why Tiger's become one of the best clutch putters ever to play the game. As he demonstrated on the final day of the 2000 PGA Championship, when the tournament hangs in the balance, Tiger finds ways to make putts he doesn't necessarily make during the earlier rounds.

I have a theory about why this should be the case. Tiger now is exposed to lots of different ideas about putting. I see and hear things that indicate he's listening to them. He'll talk, for instance, on the day before a tournament about how he's been working on the practice green trying to make his ball roll a particular way—a way that supposedly helps it hold its line and find the hole.

But under pressure, we revert to our dominant habits. Tiger's dominant habit, as far as putting was concerned, was planted in his mind at a very early age by his father. Earl Woods has described how he taught Tiger to putt when Tiger was a toddler. Earl had Tiger put a ball in his right hand and roll it to a hole. Then he had Tiger close his eyes and roll it to the hole again.

He asked Tiger what he'd "seen" after he closed his eyes. Tiger would reply that he'd seen a "picture" of the hole.

Earl taught Tiger always to see that mental picture of the hole before he struck the ball with his putter. He taught him not to worry about the mechanics of the stroke, just to make sure he saw that target in his mind's eye before he putted the ball. He knew that Tiger's brain would take care of the rest more often than not.

It was inspired instruction. When Tiger is in clutch situations, when he falls back on his dominant habit, he's focusing tightly on his target, that picture in his mind. That's why he makes so many clutch putts. Part of Butch Harmon's genius is that, while he's worked on Tiger's full swing, he hasn't tried to change the putting concept Tiger got from his father. A lot of coaches might have fiddled with Tiger's stroke to the point that he got a new and less effective dominant habit. They might have kept Tiger from the success he's had.

Orientation toward the target works because the subconscious brain is capable of quick, accurate adjustments. That's what happens when Billy Mayfair is focused on his target. He unconsciously aims a little left, then squares the blade to the real target line just before his putter strikes the ball—sending it where he wants it to go. Suppose, instead, he was consciously thinking of pushing the putter blade straight through the line. His subconscious mind would be overridden and he'd probably pull his putt to the left. His target orientation makes him a good putter.

•   •   •

A GOOD PUTTER'S target is never simply the hole. He's always trying to putt the ball into the hole, but the hole is much too big to serve as a good target. The smaller the target you have, the better your brain and body can function in trying to get the ball there. On short putts, you should pick out the smallest target you can focus on. It might be a blade of grass or a discoloration on the edge of the hole. It might be a scuff mark on the white liner inside the hole.

I say that the brain and body "can" function well in reacting to a small target, not that they will automatically do so. Some people, as their target gets smaller, tend to get more careful and controlling with their stroke. They can make a free stroke easily if you tell them simply to putt the ball to nothing. But the smaller the target gets, the tighter they get. Putters have to overcome this. They have to discipline themselves to putt as freely to a small target as they do when they putt to nothing.

On breaking putts, the choice of target varies with individuals, but the target generally won't be in or in many cases even near the hole. I'd teach any new player to make all putts straight putts. How do you do this? Suppose you think that the putt will break about four inches from right to left. Since four inches is the approximate diameter of the cup, measure one cup width from the edge of the hole to the right and pick out a blade of grass or a discoloration there. That's your target. Sometimes, with a downhill putt on a dramatic slope, a player will pick the spot on the green that he considers the apex of the ball's curving journey to the hole. Or it might be the point where a putt reaches the crest of a downslope and starts to go downhill. It doesn't matter. Let the slope of the green and gravity break the ball into the hole.

Some very good players I've worked with have individual peculiarities in this aspect of their putting. If Nick Price has a putt he expects to break six inches, he aims six inches from the hole. But he looks at the hole just before he makes his stroke. Padraig Harrington aims at a spot a foot or so in front of the ball. Somehow, Nick's subconscious mind gets the ball started where he's aiming, not where he's looking. Padraig's subconscious mind gets the putt rolling at the right pace even though he's looking at a target only a foot in front of him. The main thing is that they are both oriented to a target.

Occasionally, our perceptions work a little differently. Most players tell me that once in a while, when they start to examine a putt, they see a line. This perception has different looks for different people. Some say it reminds them of the tracks in the morning dew that golf balls sometimes make. Some say it's like a thin line. Some see a wide line. I've also had players tell me they imagine a line of buried ball magnets under the green, drawing their ball inexorably toward the cup.

Some people seem to have a little movie projector running in their minds. They see the ball rolling toward its target and into the hole. Some see a fragment of that—the first two feet of the ball's journey, or the last two feet.

All of these sorts of perceptions are fine, as long as whatever they're imagining—the line, the magnets, etc.—leads to a target.

Don't be concerned if you rarely or never see a line, or if your brain doesn't furnish you with a "coming attractions" clip of the putt you're about to make. That doesn't mean you're not a good putter. It simply means that your brain doesn't work as visually as some other people's. Don't try to force yourself to see a line. Picking out a target and believing that it will work is equally effective.

If you do see a line, don't be afraid to use it. It's probably a very good representation of what the ball will actually do. If you see such lines all the time, count your blessings. It can help you putt more decisively.

There's only one problem that orientation to a line can lead to, and it's analogous to the problem some players have when they select a small target and tighten up. A player can be too careful about trying to start the ball out along the line he has imagined. He can try to steer the blade of the putter along the line.

That doesn't work. Steering the putter, being too careful, strips a player of much of his natural ability and accuracy. It interferes with the purity of the interaction between a target and the nervous system. Human beings are wired to putt best when the golfer simply sees the target and reacts to it with as little conscious thought as possible.

Brad Faxon, who's one of the best putters in the world, is one of those people who generally "sees" a line when he examines a putt. But Brad doesn't try to force the ball along this line. He simply lets the putt go and trusts that his subconscious will get it moving along the line he's "seen."

I often compare it to the way athletes in other sports react to targets. A basketball player doesn't leap into the air, eye the basket, and then ponder how best to set his wrist to get off a good shot. He jumps, sees the target, and lets the shot go. A football quarterback, faced with blitzing linebackers, doesn't give himself a lecture on how to throw tight spirals. He looks to where the receiver is going to be, focuses on that spot, and drills the ball there. That's the way good putters operate, too. Putting well is very athletic.

The analogy to basketball and football targets raises another issue. I sometimes hear television commentators talk about trying to lag a long putt into a three-foot circle around the hole. I have never understood the logic behind this idea. Would a basketball player improve his chances of making a three-point shot if he aimed for the backboard instead of the basket? Would a quarterback do well if he threw the ball somewhere in the general direction of his receiver?

Of course not. Yet I often hear golfers being advised that when they're thirty feet or more from the hole, the best thing to do is draw that imaginary circle around the hole and just try to get the ball into it. I can think of only two reasons for the popularity of this idea. One is that golfers found it easier to make a free, confident stroke if they thought that all they had to do was get the ball into a three-foot circle. The other is that the commentators and teachers themselves thought this way when they were playing tournament golf. This makes an ironic sort of sense. If you try to putt into a three-foot circle, you're only going to increase your margin of error. Instead of being a couple of feet from the hole, your first putts are going to end up four and five feet away. You're going to be missing a few of those second putts. And, if you're a tournament golfer and you three-putt very often, you're soon going to be looking for another line of work—like being a television commentator or teacher.

The advocates of the three-foot circle may think what they really mean is that it's smart to play conservatively, especially in the first few rounds of a tournament. A generation ago, that's what some very good golfers did. Their objective in the first round of a U.S. Open, for instance, was not to "shoot themselves out of it" by turning in a 77 or 78. They didn't really start trying to hole all their putts until the back nine on Sunday afternoon.

Whether or not that was sound strategy thirty years ago, it certainly isn't a winning idea today. Golf, like most sports, has gotten more competitive. A player who shoots even par for the first two or three rounds of a professional event, a major championship, or even an elite amateur competition will quite likely be so far behind the leaders that it doesn't matter what he does on the back nine on Sunday. That's the way tournament golf is nowadays. If you aren't trying to hole every putt you have, you are going to lose to someone who is.

To win in golf today, you have to be prepared to go low at every opportunity. By low, I mean shooting not just in the 60s, but the low 60s. Obviously, to go low a player must be in command of his entire game—driving the ball well, hitting greens, sinking putts. Of the three, the last is the most important. Quite often, professional golfers get their swings grooved well enough that they have a chance to go low. The ones who actually do it are the ones who are able to discipline their minds to think only of the target at every putting opportunity. The ones who fail to go low let other thoughts get in their way. They think that they've already gotten three or four under par, so they ought to be careful and preserve their subpar finish. Or they think they're not good enough to shoot a 64 in competition. Or they think they've used up their birdie putts for the day, as if some government bureaucracy had issued each player the same daily quota.

I work with a player named Tripp Isenhour who's had that problem. When Tripp was at Georgia Tech, he was a good, consistent college golfer. He never shot a high round. He didn't shoot many particularly low rounds either. Once he turned pro, though, he found that shooting a couple of rounds of even par was a good way to have weekends off and go broke fast. Tripp actually quit golf in frustration a few years ago and went to work in his family's Christmas tree business in North Carolina.

When he decided to give professional golf another shot,

Tripp and I worked hard on his attitude toward putting, particularly on thinking of the target and only the target. He had to learn that seeing the target and reacting to it meant that he was doing his best. He had to learn to be content with that, even on days when all of his putts didn't fall, and particularly on days when nothing fell on the first four or five holes. Tripp accepted these ideas. That, along with a serious commitment to fitness, practice, and a lot of other good habits, helped improve his game. He made it to the Buy.com Tour after a year's time. He set his sights on the ultimate goal of becoming a winner on the PGA Tour.

I knew he was getting there when he called and let me know how he'd won the Mississippi Golf Coast Open a few months ago. Tripp shot 70-75 and barely made the cut. In the third round, the field faced miserable weather conditions, wet and windy.

But that was the day Tripp discovered that his game was under control and he had a chance to go low. He seized that opportunity.

He birdied five of the first six holes, sinking putts from four feet to thirty feet. He was seeing his target, having no trouble believing in it. His touch was just right.

"Let's keep it going, keep rolling it to the target," he told himself. "Relax and let it happen."

He fended off thoughts of how far under par he was or what the rest of the field was doing, and where he stood in the tournament. Only later that day, after his round was over, would he learn that just one other player managed to break 70. He just kept seeing his target and rolling his ball to it.

Tripp didn't make all his putts that day. In fact, he lipped out six of them. But his mental discipline stayed intact through all eighteen holes. At day's end, he had a 63. He won that tournament on the strength of that low round. And that victory helped assure him of a promotion to the PGA Tour the following year.

The key to all of that was clearing his mind and thinking only of his target.

Gaining Control by
Giving Up Control

*I would like to be able to knock in as many
putts as Billy does, but even more than that, I
would like to be able to act like he does when
he's doing it—with an air of unconcern as to
whether the putt drops or not.*

—ARNOLD PALMER, SPEAKING OF BILLY CASPER

UNLESS YOU'VE STEEPED YOURSELF IN THE HISTORY OF GOLF, YOU'VE
probably never heard of Wild Bill Mehlhorn. Obscurity is the
fate of poor putters.

In his day, Bill Mehlhorn may have been as good a striker of
the golf ball as ever lived. No less an authority than Ben Hogan
said Mehlhorn was the best he'd ever seen from tee to green. If
Hogan thought Bill Mehlhorn was the best ball striker he'd ever
seen, and most people think Hogan was the best ball striker
golf has ever seen, where does that put Mehlhorn?

To Hogan, though, the archetypal Bill Mehlhorn hole was a
par-4 they played together in a tournament long ago. Mehlhorn
drove the ball beautifully on this hole, long and straight. He

striped an iron to within two feet of the cup. And he played his fourth shot from a bunker.

No wonder they called him Wild Bill.

In his old age, Mehlhorn reminisced about his golf career. He recalled that he was one of those players who let his skill at hitting the ball put more and more pressure on his putting, since he knew that it was only putting that separated him from Bobby Jones, Gene Sarazen, and Walter Hagen, the leading golfers of his era. He recalled that on the tee and in the fairways, he was always relaxed and confident. But on the greens, he had a different mentality. He played not with confidence but with desperate desire. This desire drove him to think incessantly about his putting stroke, to try to force himself to putt well.

In the end, that drove him out of tournament golf, despite his lovely full swing. It's a syndrome that, if anything, has grown more widespread in the years since Wild Bill Mehlhorn played tournament golf. I've met many players who fight it.

When I meet with new clients on a practice green it's generally quite easy to persuade them that clearing their minds and thinking only of their targets improves their putting. More often than not, a professional golfer with a clear mind and a focus on a target will hole nearly all of his five-footers, lots of ten- to fifteen-footers, and a fair number of even longer putts. He'll turn to me with a pleased smile and say, "Gee, Doc, I putt really well when you're standing here. I never knew it could be this easy."

It's not.

All too often that player who putted so well on the practice green will come in after his next tournament round with a 73 or 74 next to his name. He'll tell me that he can't understand what happened to his putting. "I was trying hard, really hard, to clear my mind and think only of my target," he will say. "But it didn't work. No matter how much I was grinding away at it, I still couldn't make any putts."

As soon as I hear the word *grinding,* I have a good idea of what went wrong.

Grinding is one of those concepts that is widespread in sport and, unfortunately, inimical to good putting.

Grinding suggests that someone is doing his utmost to succeed. If he's weight training, he's popping capillaries to make sure he gets that last repetition done. If we're talking about football, we're talking about a team that keeps the ball on the ground, blocks fiercely, runs hard, and scores touchdowns by stringing together four-yard gains up the middle. If we're talking about a student, we're talking about someone who might not have the highest SAT scores in his class, but who closes the library every night because he's going to get into medical school no matter what.

And if he's putting, it suggests that he's trying to *will* the ball into the hole.

I generally admire grinders, and I believe in the transcendent importance of will. Free will is a precious, fundamental part of human nature, the part on which all true accomplishment is based. A strong will is very helpful in putting. But it's helpful only when you're behind the ball, preparing to putt. Will helps you discipline yourself to eliminate distractions and pick out a target. Will helps you work on that part of the putting process until you firmly believe in your target, believe that if you roll the ball to it, the ball will go in the hole. Pat Bradley, who has one of the strongest wills I have ever encountered, told me once that she felt as if her mind was burning a line between the ball and the hole.

But the application of will gets trickier when you are standing over the ball, ready to putt it. In fact, I believe that at that point, will can get in the way. The proper role for a strong will at this stage of putting is to support a firm belief in the golfer's mind that all the preparation is done and the ball will go in the hole if he turns control of the action over to his subconscious. But then free will must exit the stage and leave the scene to other actors.

I have heard players say that they will the ball into the hole, and some of them have been successful putters. I believe that their will helps them focus their attention on their targets and eliminate all other thoughts. But if they then continue to try to force themselves, through an act of will, to hit a perfect putt, I think any success they have is a tribute to their innate ability, their concentration, and their belief in their targets. I think they could putt even better if they stopped being so willful when they stroked their putts.

Paul Azinger is a great example. Long before he ever talked to me about his putting, Paul had been an extremely successful player, winning lots of Tour events, a PGA Championship, and contributing to some memorable and emotional Ryder Cup wins. He displayed the strength of his will again when he battled and defeated cancer.

When we started working together, Paul told me that despite all his success, he'd never actually liked the way his putting felt. To him, it wasn't athletic, free, or easy. He felt that he had an artificial stroke, one that he mechanically forced into the pattern he'd been taught was classic—a short backswing, a long follow-through, and a putter head that accelerated through the ball.

I could see that tension, that artificiality, in his stroke. In fact, I could hear it. Forced strokes look different from free strokes, and the contact between putter and ball actually sounds different.

I told Paul that his putting didn't seem to fit with the rest of his game. When he was in a bunker, for instance, he hit beautifully athletic, relaxed shots that had more than once gone into the cup to win a tournament for him. How, I asked him, did he think about his bunker shots?

"It's like night and day from my putting stroke," he said. "I don't think about it. I just look where I want it to go, splash the sand, and it goes there."

Paul did not need me to spell out for him the obvious fact that if he wanted his putting to be as outstanding as his bunker play, he had to attain the same mental state on the greens that he had in the bunkers. He had to become relaxed, even nonchalant at the moment of truth. This can be very tough to do, especially if a golfer has already mastered the idea of picking out a small target. Picking out a minute target makes a lot of golfers want to make their strokes minutely precise. The challenge of putting consists essentially of doing the opposite— picking out a small target and then taking a free, uncontrolled stroke.

I suggested that Paul think about gaining control by giving up control.

This can be a hard concept to grasp. Players are told that putting is crucially important. They're told they can't win if they don't putt well. They understand that both of those statements are true. Then they're told that at the very climax of their putting routines, they can't try very hard. They hear words and phrases like *nonchalant, carefree, don't give a damn.* I tell them to putt as if they didn't care whether they made it or not. Or to putt as if it had been preordained that the ball would fall no matter how they stroked it.

A lot of players respond to that by saying, "Huh?"

I remind them of a few things. How well do they do with four-footers if they're in a stroke-play competition where every putt counts? How well do they do with four-footers when they're out with their friends playing a casual Nassau and someone concedes that four-footer? They miss a lot of the four-footers that count. When they take a casual swipe at the putt that's been conceded, they knock it in with remarkable frequency.

I remind them that even if they could somehow force their

body to do everything perfectly, they still couldn't will the ball into the hole. Putting machines hitting balls on flat greens still miss a fair number of putts. There are just too many variables that are beyond control. The turf can be imperfect. The ball can be imperfect. The wind can gust. Any of these factors can cause a putt to miss.

But the main reason trying too hard doesn't work is that it almost invariably diminishes the chance of making a good stroke. It introduces doubt to the mind. It tightens the muscles. It robs a player of his natural talent and destroys his rhythm and flow.

Sometimes an example from another sport helps golfers see this. In basketball, for example, I've noticed that teams often play better defense when they're on the end of the floor where their bench is. But they play better offense on the opposite end. The reason is that their coach is yelling at them and they hear him. This raises their intensity on defense. Intense defenders are generally better defenders than casual ones.

On offense, the coach's voice can also raise intensity. But that rarely results in more scoring. On the offensive end, a basketball team doesn't need feverish intensity. It needs creativity, boldness, imagination, and confidence. It needs players who keep looking for their shot even when they've missed a few. When the coach is haranguing his players to work harder on offense, he's not going to get more points. He's going to get more turnovers, more missed shots, and more foregone opportunities.

But the coach doesn't stop yelling, often for the worst of reasons. He knows that to most of the people in the stands and the writers on press row, a coach who's always on his feet, always telling his players something, is perceived as an admirable character. He's showing dedication. He's showing he cares. A coach who sits back and says very little during the course of a game had better have a good team. Otherwise, critics will call him lackadaisical.

Each golfer has his own internal coach. And he's tempted to unleash that coach, to tell himself to try his best when he's putting, even though he might know it's counterproductive. That's because we've been conditioned since childhood to believe that losing isn't pleasant. But it's at least acceptable if the athlete gave 100 percent of himself. I've had players tell me that they can live with themselves if they try hard and putt poorly. But they can't sleep at night if they putt poorly and have the sense that they weren't trying hard enough. They don't understand that the only relationship between trying your hardest and doing your best is that if you try your hardest you won't do your best—in putting, at least.

The most persuasive thing I can say to someone who doesn't get this idea is, "Well, if what you've been doing had been working, we wouldn't be talking, would we?" I don't say it to be harsh, but because I know that old and destructive habits of thought are like weeds. They're hard to kill.

Gaining control by giving up control only seems like a contradiction in terms. In fact, it's a fairly common pattern in our lives.

Take, for instance, a teenager. There comes a time in a teen's life when his or her parents have to understand that they can no longer have complete control over their child's life. They can't dictate where she is at every moment, whom she speaks to, what she wears, what she does. If they try to dictate these details, the teenager is likely to rebel and, behind the parents' backs, do exactly what they don't want. Parents of teenagers are much wiser if they relax the reins and trust that the years they spent instilling sense and values into their child's mind will pay off when they give the child some independence.

Putting is like that.

Take, for instance, a public speaker. When an inexperienced speaker is asked to make a presentation before an audience, it's usually because someone admires her mind and figures she has something worthwhile to say, that she's a person of accomplishment. Being an accomplished person, this inexperienced speaker sets out to eliminate the possibility that she'll stand up behind the lectern, open her mouth, and not be able to think of anything to say. She wants desperately to avoid that. So she writes her speech down, word for word. She edits it. She memorizes it. She practices it. And when the time comes to deliver the speech, just to make sure she won't leave anything out or stand up and draw a blank, she brings her text and reads it. And, of course, she reads it so dully that the admirable qualities of mind that caused her to be invited in the first place never come across to her audience.

I'm fortunate in that I once had a teacher, June Dorian, who advised me to approach a public presentation as if I were having a conversation with one person—casual, relaxed, engaged.

Putting is like that, too.

Take, for instance, jazz musicians. Good jazz men relax. They let the music flow. They don't get hung up on playing every note of a song exactly as the composer wrote it. They don't care if being free costs them an occasional riff that doesn't work. They know that if they want the piano to sing, they have to let it go.

Putting is like that, too.

Take for instance, dancing. A lot of people think they can't dance. But they go to a family wedding, have a couple of drinks, start feeling the music, and dance very well. They may wake up the next morning with a hangover. And they may still believe they can't dance. But when the video of the wedding reception is played, the truth is evident. They can dance if they let themselves not care about dancing correctly.

Putting is like that.

Or, consider your signature. If you're signing checks on bill-paying day, the likelihood is that each of your signatures is basically identical to the others. But suppose I were to hand you a blank piece of paper and say, "Here. Sign this paper exactly as you signed those checks. If the signature doesn't seem genuine to an FBI handwriting expert, you owe me $10,000."

The likelihood is that you would try *very* hard to make your signature identical to the one on the checks. And precisely because you were trying hard, it would not be. It would lack the casual flow your signature usually has. The lines would look wiggly, forced. It would look, in short, like a forgery.

Putting is like that.

Still, when I explain all this to a player and urge him to try gaining control by giving up control, the player sometimes gets the sense that I'm suggesting he not care. And how can he not care about a vitally important part of the game he loves, the game he must play well to fulfill his dreams and support his family?

The answer, of course, is that I'm not asking players to stop caring. I'm asking them to give themselves their best chance to make putts. And the best way to do this is to relax a little, perhaps even to pretend they don't care, to remind themselves that even if they miss a crucial putt, the bank is not going to foreclose and their kids will still love them. Minimizing the importance of a putt is much more helpful than maximizing it.

Paul Azinger immediately grasped the idea of gaining control by giving up control. It appealed to him. Some players respond to one idea, others to another. You have to find a way to present an idea in a way that seems to the player instinctive and understandable to him. For Paul, that was "gain control by giving up control."

We started working on a few putting drills. I asked him to keep his eyes on his target as he began to draw his putter back. He did. I asked him to keep in mind the idea of gaining control by giving up control. He did.

"That feels so free, so flowing," he said, pleased.

I could see the difference in his stroke. It was longer, but it didn't look artificial. It looked better. Contact between ball and putter sounded quieter. The ball seemed to roll a foot or two farther than he expected. (I suspect the changes in the sound and the distance the ball traveled were because a free, unforced stroke is more likely to contact the ball precisely on the putter's sweet spot.)

Not long after that, Paul won his first tournament since his bout with cancer. He's playing very well now, and he's near the top of the Tour's putting statistics. He tells me he's putting every putt as if the guys playing with him had already conceded it.

Other players grasp the concept in different ways. When I started working with Nick Price, one of the problems we confronted was that Nick felt his putting stroke was forced on putts in the ten-foot range. But he really liked his stroke and his mind-set when he putted from twenty to forty feet or more.

The reason, of course, was that Nick felt he should make and had to make the ten-footers. He didn't expect to make the longer putts. When he lined them up, he visualized them going into the hole. But he could live with it if they didn't. So he stroked them more casually—and better. It wasn't that he wasn't trying to make them. He was. But he relaxed on the longer putts because he didn't care so much.

Nick and I worked on making him putt as if every putt was a forty-footer. That was one of the stories behind the story when Nick became player of the year in 1994. He was trying to putt everything as if it was a forty-footer.

No one believes he can will the ball into the hole from forty feet. Good putters try to make their forty-footers. But they understand that their efforts will come up against the vagaries of wind and slope, and the imperfections of turf. They understand that the human body and mind aren't precise enough to hole all forty-footers. So they putt the ball as well as they can and they are phlegmatic if it fails to drop.

That's the way I like players to be about all their putts, even the short ones. Take your satisfaction not from whether the putt drops but from whether you got yourself into the right frame of mind before you hit it. Make the putt in your mind. If you do that, you have done all you can. It's up to fate whether the ball actually drops.

That doesn't mean golfers should be careless about their putting. In fact, I appreciate a meticulous putter. But the smart putter is meticulous to a certain point. She's meticulous about the process of preparing for a putt. She has a routine, and she executes that routine.

But at the moment of truth, she stops being meticulous and simply strokes the putt, freely and even nonchalantly. She expects the ball to go in the hole, but she understands that sometimes it won't.

If you'd like a little jargon from modern psychology, try the phrase *process goals*. By process goals, we mean the preparatory things an individual can do to maximize the chance of peak performance in any endeavor, whether it be selling stocks and bonds or making putts. We don't mean results.

To the financial consultant, the process that leads to success involves first preparing himself, from his wardrobe to his knowledge of the market. It involves preparing his presentation. It involves preparing lists of prospects. It involves finding out as much as he can about each prospect before he calls on him. It involves executing his presentation plan.

But once he's gone through this process as well as he can, the successful financial consultant knows that some prospects are going to say yes and some are going to say no. He can't control what the prospect says. He can only control the process he goes through. If the prospect says yes, the consultant is gratified. But if the prospect says no, the successful financial consultant doesn't worry about it. He reviews his performance, checks to make sure he fulfilled his process goals. And if he did, he simply looks forward to the next call, the next prospect. If he has any reaction at all, he thinks, Good. Everyone's got to hear no sometimes. This just brings me that much closer to the prospect who will say yes.

The good putter thinks similarly. If he misses a putt, he reviews his performance. Did he clear his mind of all thoughts but the target? Did he make a free, confident stroke? If he did, he did all he could do. If he still missed, he just mentally shrugs his shoulders. If all putts went in, he figures, golf would be too easy. That miss just makes it all the more likely that he'll make the next one.

The player who hasn't learned to gain control by giving up control doesn't have that edge working for him. He cares much more about the result of his putt than the process that produced it. He's the sort of player who talks to himself a lot on the green, who's got no consistency as a putter. Especially when he misses some putts on the first few holes, he has no discipline. He reacts to missed putts by altering his approach. He fiddles with his grip and his stance. He overreads his putts. He overcontrols his stroke. And he loses, still thinking he can somehow find a way to force himself to hit perfect putts.

Making Putts Routinely

*If there has been one thing common to all
great putters over the years, it has been their
determination to stick with one method and
one overall game plan through thick and
thin.*

—Paul Runyan

IF YOU GO TO A PGA TOUR EVENT WHERE MY FRIEND AND CLIENT
Davis Love III is playing, I suggest you stake out the practice
green and wait till he arrives. You'll be able to pick up a quick
lesson in one of the elements that makes a good putter.

I'm not talking about watching Davis's stroke, though it's a
good one. Watch the number of balls he's hitting. A lot of players take three or more balls onto the practice green. They hit
one toward a hole, rake the second into place, hit it, and rake
the third into place. Not Davis. He always practices putting with
a single ball. After he hits it, he walks to it and either hits it again
or picks it up and locates another target. Then he repeats the
process.

I point this out not because of any inherent magic in using a single ball on the practice green, but because it illustrates Davis's commitment to his putting routine. He wants to practice the same routine he uses on the golf course, and on the golf course, he has only one ball. That devotion to an unvarying routine is one of the hallmarks of a good putter. Davis, who is a very good putter, employs the same routine whenever he putts, whether it's in a practice round or on the final green at the Belfry with the Ryder Cup at stake.

If you continue to watch Davis, you'll soon be able to predict exactly what he will do before he strokes each practice putt. You'll even be able to tell how much time will elapse between each movement he makes. A good putter's routine can be that predictable.

Developing a good routine was one of the first things Davis and I worked on when we met years ago. He was in college, and his father, Davis Love Jr., was concerned that Davis wasn't putting or chipping as well as he needed to. Young Davis wanted to be a great player, but he didn't think he was much of a putter.

I could see otherwise. Davis had talent as a putter. But, as I told him, he was getting in his own way.

In this context, getting in your own way means permitting something extraneous that you generate to interfere with putting your best. If a player is about to putt and he starts silently lecturing himself about taking the putter head straight back along the target line, he's getting in his own way. If he remembers the putts of similar length that he's missed in the past, he's getting in his own way. If he starts wondering whether he can make the cut if he misses the putt, he's getting in his own way. If he starts thinking about how much money is at stake, or whether someone else is making birdies, he's getting in his own way.

Most golfers face a constant battle to stay out of their own way. One of their allies in this struggle is a strong putting routine. A putting routine has two intertwined components. One is the physical activity—taking the grip, taking the stance, practice swings, etc. The second, and more important, component is the mental activity—reading the green, deciding on the line, clearing the mind, putting to make it, and accepting the results.

We are creatures of habit. A good, habitual putting routine helps us stay out of our own way much as a regular exercise habit protects against heart problems. It's not foolproof, but it's the wise thing to do.

It wasn't hard to persuade Davis about this. We just watched some sports on television. If you look closely at them, you can see that successful athletes in many situations similar to a golfer's rely on habit and routine. We watched Michael Jordan of North Carolina and Mark Price of Georgia Tech shoot free throws. They each had a ritual way of taking the ball from the referee, taking their stance, warming up by dribbling or spinning the ball in their hands, taking aim, and letting the shot go. We saw the analogous thing with placekickers in football and servers in tennis.

I pointed out that at the heart of Jordan's and Price's routines, there was something in common. Both Jordan and Price moved decisively at the moment of truth. They looked at the target and let the shot go without delay. It was much the same when we watched Larry Bird win the NBA's three-point shooting contest. Larry grabbed balls off the rack quickly and decisively. He focused on the target and let the shots go without wasting time. There was no sign that he cared about his shooting form.

Davis could see parallels to other sports that he liked. He's an avid fisherman. We talked about how when he saw fish biting at some remove from his boat, Davis simply looked at where he wanted his lure to go and cast it there. He didn't think about wrist cock, or where the pole was aimed. He just saw it and did it. If, one time out of fifteen, the lure didn't go where he was aiming, he didn't reprove himself or start studying his technique. He just cast again.

Davis also likes to hunt. He was reminded of a man who taught trap and skeet-shooting at Sea Island, Georgia, where Davis lived. This expert taught novice shooters not to think about aiming the gun. They had to watch for the target, focus on the target, and fire. It's a fluid motion. The gun is never still until the trigger has been pulled.

Davis still had trouble thinking of himself as a good enough athlete to apply this idea to putting. I had him toss a ball to me. Unconsciously, of course, he tossed it precisely into my hand.

"That shows you're athlete enough to putt," I said. "Now you have to trust that a very smart engineer designed your putter to fit in your hands, to hit the ball straight. You shouldn't have to think about that any more than you think about your hand when you toss me the ball. In fact, you can putt a lot better with your putter than you can rolling the ball with your hand."

Davis set about mastering a routine that captured his athleticism. It took hundreds and hundreds of repetitions before it became unconscious and automatic, but once Davis makes a commitment to something, he sticks to it. That's why he began working with a single ball on the practice green, and why he always practices the same rhythmic core of his routine. He looks at the target. He looks at the ball. And he strokes his putt as soon as his eyes come back to the ball. It's a routine designed to maximize the chance that he will putt with no extraneous thoughts getting in his way.

Not coincidentally, Davis transformed himself from a young man who didn't think he was much of a putter to a mature golfer who is perennially near the top of the Tour's putting statistics.

You are going to have to develop and consistently employ a sound routine if you are going to become the best putter you can be. If you do, I can offer you this guarantee. On your good days, you will putt great. On your bad days, you'll putt pretty well. That's how powerful a good routine is.

Some readers will react to this by thinking, That's crazy. I play all the time with guys who have elaborate putting routines that they always follow, and they putt poorly and can't break 90!

Well, then, evidently they are not employing the sort of routine I'm talking about. They may have a set of motions that they execute. They may squat down behind the ball the same way, plumb-bob the same way, take their stance and grip the same way, take the same number of practice strokes, and take the same deep breath on every putt. But the physical elements, as I've mentioned, are only one component of a good routine, and by no means the most important one. Players who move their bodies through a routine but fail to get their minds where they must be are like people who go to church every Sunday but sit there thinking about work, school, sex, or golf—anything but faith and prayer. God, I assume, is less than impressed by that sort of devotion. In the same way, your putting will not be transformed if you adopt a shallow, purely physical routine.

It's the mental part of a routine that's more difficult to master. Anyone can move his body through a prescribed ritual. But the discipline required to be in the right frame of mind on every putt is difficult to achieve and easy to lose. I work with more than one player on the Tour who fights a constant battle to clarify his thoughts, to see only the target, to think only of the target, and then to let the stroke happen.

That's not to say that a consistent physical routine isn't helpful. It is. Body and mind are part of a unified system, and a sound set of physical habits can promote and support sound mental habits.

I almost never try to prescribe the physical routine. I've seen too many good putters whose routines vary widely from one another to think that there's a single correct way. Some plumb-bob. Some don't. Some squat behind the ball. Some don't. Some take their practice strokes standing behind the ball, looking at the hole, swinging perpendicular to the line of the putt. Some take practice strokes parallel to the line of the putt. Some take the same number of practice strokes before every putt. Some take no practice strokes at all. Some take a varying number of practice strokes, depending on how long it takes them to feel that they've rehearsed the correct stroke for the putt they have to make. It doesn't matter. People's styles differ because people differ. The main thing is to have a physical routine that feels comfortable and effective to you. Then stick with it.

At the core of the routine, though, are some physical movements that I think are less open to individual interpretation. When the moment of truth comes, I like to see players look at the target, look at the ball, and let the stroke go, with no delay between those three movements.

When I see a player who looks at the target, looks back at the ball, and then freezes, I can generally guess what's going on in his mind. He's giving himself a lecture on the putting stroke. Or he's trying to remember the latest tip he saw on television. He is getting in his own way. He is also drastically reducing his chance to make the putt. That's because every instant spent frozen over the ball, thinking about technique or anything else but the target, is an instant in which the body can tense up, the nerves and muscles can get less graceful, and the mind can lose its focus. For every instant frozen over the ball, the golfer is less likely to simply see it and do it.

So I like to see a smooth, relaxed cadence to a player's routine at this point. Sometimes I have them murmur to themselves, "Look at the target. Look at the ball. Roll it." It's interesting that when they slur the endings of each of those sentences so that they sound more like "look at the targetlook at the ballroll it," their putting usually becomes still sharper.

Cindy Figg-Currier, who plays on the LPGA Tour, carries a small metronome to the practice green with her. Sometimes, in drills, she sets it up and starts it ticking with a slow, steady beat. She strokes putts to the sound of that metronome. She feels it helps maintain the smoothness of her stroke. It also helps her maintain the right rhythm in her routine.

The physical elements of a good putting routine won't help you, though, if your mental routine is weak.

THE MENTAL ROUTINE can actually begin before a player arrives on the green, when the player begins to read his putt. The eyes and mind of a good player start to process information about a putt almost as soon as his approach shot stops moving. As he strides up the fairway toward the hole, his imagination comes into play. He sees the general contour of the land and he starts to envision how his ball will be affected when he rolls it.

Much has been written over the years about reading putts. Some of it is no doubt valid, but a lot of it is pseudo-science at best. One thing I do know is that I've seen a lot of putts missed because golfers' heads were churning with so much "information" about how to read greens that they were unable to focus on their targets.

Where does the green drain? What's the grain of the grass? What percentage of putts don't break at all? What percentage of golfers underread their putts and what percentage overread them? What's the effect of footprints around the hole? Has the architect built any optical illusions into this green? If you're thinking about this sort of question, you're likely to be filling your mind with thoughts and doubts that won't help you sink your putt.

This leads to an irony. Experience often doesn't help much in reading putts. It's the older, more experienced players who have had time to absorb all the supposedly helpful data about reading greens who tend to become paralyzed by doubt. Kids who are new to the game seem to know better. I attend a fair number of junior golf tournaments, and I can tell you that kids read greens remarkably well. And they know nothing about grain, drainage, or any of the other supposed fine points of reading putts. They just take a look and whack it.

They putt well in that unsophisticated way because they tend to go with their first impression of how the putt will break. If I have a cardinal rule about reading greens, that's it. Your first impression of how a putt will break will be right more often than any other impression you might form.

That doesn't mean you must read the putt the instant you step onto the green. Cindy Figg-Currier has a useful metaphor in this regard. She tells me that she thinks of reading putts as a process similar to focusing a camera. For those of you who can't remember the era before autofocus, you point the camera at the subject and at first get a fuzzy image. You work the focusing ring back and forth until the image is sharp and clear. But after you've done that, you don't keep turning the focusing ring, blurring and sharpening the subject again and again. Once you've got it clear, you stick with it. That's the way you should read putts.

Good putters can take in an enormous amount of information in this process. First of all, there's the memory they have of playing a particular green before. If you play regularly on the same course, over time you become familiar with the greens. When you walk onto the putting surface you may already know how a putt will break. That's fine. Local knowledge is a great advantage.

Players on the PGA Tour, who play a new course every week, try to compensate for local knowledge during their practice rounds early in the week. If you watch a practice round, you'll see that the players generally play their ball into the hole cut on that particular day. But before they leave the green, they'll putt three or four balls to different areas of the putting surface, especially those areas where they anticipate the pins will be cut. Frequently, they'll mark up the green diagrams in their yardage books with little arrows helping them to identify the contours and breaks in a green. Tour caddies pride themselves in stockpiling data about the greens on Tour courses.

That brings up an issue that sometimes confronts amateurs,

especially women—should they read the putts, should the caddie read the putts, or should it be a collaborative process?
Women tell me that they frequently encounter unenlightened
caddies who assume they can't read greens and start trying to
impose their judgments without being asked. The best thing to
do with a caddie like that is take him aside and tell him firmly
that when you'd like his advice, you'll ask for it.

On the other hand, I've had players tell me they putt better at
a club they've never played before if they take a caddie and let
him apply his experience and local knowledge to the reading
of the putt. That may be so, and I generally tend to believe in
whatever works for an individual player.

But keep several things in mind before you decide what role
you want a caddie to play in reading your putts. One is that
you're not going to get better at reading greens if you let a caddie do it for you, any more than you're going to learn to fly an
airplane by sitting in a first-class seat and letting the pilot handle it. Another is that the goal of your reading routine is to come
up with a firm, decisive idea of how the putt will break. That's
more likely to happen if only one mind is applied to the problem, rather than two. Finally, there is no single correct line for
most putts. There are many lines, depending on the speed with
which the player hits the ball. A caddie who looks at a putt and
tells you "two cups left to right" is merely displaying his igno-
rance of the game if he doesn't know how hard you plan to hit
the ball.

On the Tour, where caddies work for one player only and

can learn that player's idiosyncrasies, effective partnerships are more likely. Glen Day, for instance, has had the same caddie, Dave "Munster" Munce, for more than ten years. Glen generally likes to putt so that the ball dies in the hole. Munster has learned that, and he reads putts accordingly. The two of them have also learned over the years how to trust one another's judgment and how to say the sorts of things that produce a decisive consensus about the way a putt will break. Glen is generally the first to say how he thinks a putt will go. Munster says nothing till Glen has either stated his opinion or asks for Munster's. Nine times out of ten, Munster agrees with Glen's first impression. If Munster disagrees with Glen's impression, Glen starts the process again, and he works it till he arrives at a firm read.

But the partnership between Glen and Munster, I find, tends to be the exception nowadays. Most tour players read their own putts and rarely ask advice from their caddies.

And Tour caddies are the best in their business. What sort of partnership will you achieve with the guy that a caddie master assigns you on a given Saturday? There are going to be days when you get a new, inexperienced caddie or one who simply can't read greens. There are going to be many days when you play a course without caddies. In those circumstances you had better be able to rely on your own green-reading skills.

A related question sometimes arises over whether to watch the putts of other players in your group for clues about how your ball will break. To be sure, good players sometimes go to school on the putts hit by their competitors. But the smart ones are very selective about whom they watch.

Dottie Pepper, for instance, tells me that she sometimes watches a fellow LPGA player's putt to get a clue about the way the green will break her own putt. But she never watches the amateurs whom she plays with in pro-ams before the formal tournament begins. Their putting, she thinks, is so unlike her own that she'll more likely be misled than informed by anything she sees them do.

That's not a bad rule of thumb. A weak player in your foursome, even if he's on your line, is likely to hit the ball with either too much pace or not enough. That's one reason he's a weak player. In either case, the weak player's ball will break differently from the smart, properly paced putt you plan to hit. I've seen a lot of putts missed by players who turn to someone else in their foursome and say, "But yours broke a foot!"

I LIKE TO see players make their reads fairly quickly. Once in a while, with a long putt on a modern green that has some artificial humps, tiers, and ridges, it may be advisable to walk around a putt and see it from both sides of the hole. Do it only if you're certain that you're trying to find a way to get the ball in the hole, not looking for reasons why that's going to be hard to do. And don't do it very often. Most putts aren't that complicated.

That's not to say that you should rush through this phase of your routine. There's an understandable concern among many golfers about the pace of play these days. But it's important to realize that the problem of five-hour rounds doesn't stem from people taking their time going through their putting routines. It stems from people not being ready when it's their turn to play. It stems from course operators who insist that all players take golf carts, then that the carts remain on the cart paths. It stems from people who waste time rereading putts.

Your routine should not waste time, of course. And it must be something you can execute within the time limits allowed by the rules. But once you're confident you're within those parameters, don't let anyone or anything rush you. Go through your routine at a deliberate, comfortable pace. If you adopt a routine such as the one I've described here, you will never have trouble with slow play.

Davis Love plays a brisk round of golf. But Davis is so committed to his routine that he takes pride in stepping away and starting over if he fails to execute the mental portion of it, if he's distracted by thinking of something other than the ball going in the hole. He's got such a disciplined mind that it doesn't happen very often.

Glen Day attracted some unfavorable television commentary a few years ago from people who thought he took too much time. They gave him the nickname "All Day." Glen was smart enough not to let that fluster him. (In fact, when the company that makes his golf balls asked what name he wanted stamped on them, he told them to put "All Day" on each of them.) He goes through his routine at the pace that ensures he makes the most putts he's capable of making. When you think about it, that's a time-saving measure right there.

I don't believe much in tricks or gimmicks in reading putts. I know, for instance, that Bobby Locke liked to pay particular attention to the last few feet of a putt, the terrain it would cover just before it got to the hole. He reasoned that since the ball would be rolling more slowly at that stage of its journey, the contours around the hole were the most critical in trying to get it to break into the cup. That was fine for Locke, but I wouldn't teach a novice golfer to do it. I'd much prefer that the novice keep green reading as simple as possible.

There are a few exceptions. On a shaggy Bermuda green, you may have to remember to play less break than your first impression of the green contours suggested there would be. And in certain parts of the world, like the desert courses of southern California and Arizona, there may be a local peculiarity you have to keep in mind. In Scottsdale, Arizona, for instance, they say that all putts break toward Phoenix. And I've been on some greens out there where the ball looked like it would break one way, or go straight, and didn't, because of the Phoenix rule. So in those circumstances, you have to add a little compensation to your read.

It's no coincidence, though, that while all the Tour players who come to Scottsdale in January for the Phoenix Open know the Phoenix rule and observe it when they read putts, it's quite often a pro based in Scottsdale who wins the tournament. In much the same way, someone raised on the *Poa annua* greens of the West Coast has an edge in California and someone who grew up on Bermuda often wins tournaments played on Bermuda greens. The reason, I think, is that these pros are putting based on their first impressions. The visitors have to take their first impressions and adjust them. And a pure first impression is almost always better than a read produced by second thoughts.

Players who are putting well find it easier to observe this principle than players who aren't. David Duval tells me that when he shot his remarkable 59 in the final round of the Bob Hope Classic a couple of years ago, he barely looked at the final, seven-foot putt he had to make eagle, to win the tournament and to break 60. He just got an instinctive idea of how the ball was going to roll, picked out his target, and hit it there.

I know that few readers of this book will ever stand on the 18th green with a putt to break 60. But they might have putts to break 70, 80, 90, or 100. The principle remains the same. Can you read that putt and make your judgment about how it will break as instinctively as David Duval read his? Can you then stroke it as decisively as he stroked his?

Players who have been missing a lot of putts, of course, often can't tell for certain whether they missed because of a poor read or a poor stroke. They tend to compensate by being extremely careful with their reads. This doesn't work. It doesn't do much for a player's ability to predict how a putt will break. And the doubts and questions that it introduces do nothing at all for the player's putting stroke. Being overly careful with reads almost always leads to doubts and worries—and poor strokes. The player who begins reading too carefully winds up missing more putts. Soon he's not only overreading, he's fiddling with his stroke while playing competitively, trying to fix it. He's so lost he couldn't find water from a bridge.

Some players intuitively understand the advantage of trusting their first impression of a putt, the read that feels instinctive. But many don't. People in our culture have been raised to believe that second and third efforts distinguish winners from losers. They've been raised to check and double-check their math homework to make certain they got it right. If they don't check and double-check their reads, they feel guilty about not giving their best effort.

I have players tell me that they can live with themselves if they read and reread putts, then miss them. They can't live with themselves if they miss after feeling that they haven't tried hard.

"Oh," I say. "I thought we were looking for a way to make putts. Turns out we're looking for a way to avoid feeling guilty."

I tell them that putting is not math homework. Putting is a game, an imaginative, creative, athletic game. You putt best when you're feeling loose, decisive, and confident. Trusting your first impression helps you be that way. Reading and rereading greens makes it harder to get into that effective state of mind.

Sometimes a player will tell me, "Yeah, Doc, but the hole locations out on the Tour are chosen because they're in the places where your first impression is usually wrong. They're subtle. They're hard to read."

That's sometimes true. We've all seen greens on television where player after player misreads the putt the same way. Everyone plays the putt to break left, but it stays straight. Or vice versa.

If I saw evidence that players who reread the greens got that sort of putt in the hole and players who went with their first impression missed it, I might reassess my belief in the value of putting by that instinctive first impression. But I don't. I don't see any evidence that the second and third reads are any more accurate than the first. Everyone misreads certain putts, no matter how many times they read them. And when I walk a practice round with players, I often ask them to verbalize their first impression of a putt so I'll know what it is. It's amazing how accurate that impression is.

But I do see evidence that players plagued by doubt and misgivings about their reads make fewer putts than players who are decisive and confident. Players tell me about that sort of problem all the time.

The bottom line is that your first impression won't always be accurate, though it will be accurate a lot of the time. You're going to misread some putts, you're going to be fooled sometimes by a tricky green. That's the nature of the game. But your second and third impressions won't be any more accurate— indeed they'll be less so. And the stroke you make with two or three impressions rattling around in your brain will almost certainly be less decisive and less confident than the one you make if you go with your instinct.

Reading the green, of course, is not the object of the exercise.

Sinking putts is the object of the exercise. The goal in reading greens is to come to a point of clarity, a moment at which you are certain that you understand the way the ball will roll and you can make the ball roll that way. One way to know whether you're reaching that point is by gauging your reaction to missed putts. Are you shocked and surprised when the ball doesn't go in or doesn't break the way you'd expected? It sounds like a contradiction in terms, but if you're shocked and surprised when you misread a green, then you're doing a pretty good job.

IF YOU'RE EXECUTING a good mental routine, you're going to feel the atmosphere around you change. It won't, of course. But your perceptions of it will.

Players with strong putting routines tell me that they feel as if they're stepping into their own little world. It's almost like going into a bubble. Their awareness of the things around them fades as their focus on the putt they're facing tightens and intensifies. It's a pleasant place, this little world. They have the feeling they love to putt. They take great pleasure from their skill at it. They feel safe, secure, and competent. They don't care what anyone else thinks or might think about the putt they're about to hit. They are immersed in the challenge of putting it into the hole.

The climactic part of a good routine is very simple: putt to make it.

As my mother might say, "Why else would you putt?"

Unfortunately, there are lots of reasons. People putt not to three-putt. They putt to give themselves a good leave for their next putt. They putt not to go too far past the hole. They putt not to leave it short. They putt to make a good roll.

Well, you can buy a good roll in a doughnut shop. And none of those other reasons works very well, either.

Putt to make it. This means you're absolutely absorbed in this moment, no other. Nothing else in the world interests you except making this particular putt. There is no future and no past. You're not dwelling on the good shot you hit to get your ball to this spot. You're not thinking of how you'll feel if you miss. You're just rolling this ball into that hole.

Seve Ballesteros, a two-time Masters champion, once four-putted a green at Augusta. He was asked about it later in the media center. "I putt and miss. I putt and miss. I putt and miss. I putt and make," Seve explained.

People laughed, but it suggested to me something about the way Seve's mind worked. Seve's answer suggested that he was completely in the present moment on each of those putts. He didn't say that the greens at Augusta were slick and treacherous. He didn't ruminate about the iron shot that may have left him with a tough first putt. His attitude hadn't changed from one putt to the next. He wasn't affected by his misses. He had had four putts. He'd tried to make each of them. He'd succeeded on the fourth.

He had done all a golfer can do. That's why, in his prime, he was such a great player.

. . .

GOOD PUTTERS DON'T four-putt very often, but no matter how good you are, you are going to miss some putts, most likely ten or more during every round you play. A smart response to those inevitable misses is the last major element in a good routine. You must be resilient about missed putts. Remember that it's how you respond to your misses that matters, not whether you miss. You can choose to be angry about your misses or you can choose to accept them.

I don't advocate getting angry about missed putts. I've known a few players who could blow up emotionally, recover quickly, and use that anger to help become more focused for the next putt. But that ability is very rare. More often than not, anger is the enemy of focus. A temper tantrum is a form of getting in your own way.

It's important to distinguish between types of anger. If you're angry at yourself because you didn't putt to make it, that's one thing. At least you're focusing on the real mistake. If you vow to do better at focusing your mind for the next putt, a bit of what Sam Snead called "sensible irritation" might actually be helpful.

But if you get angry simply because the ball didn't go in the hole, it can lead to problems. Maybe you'll start to pity yourself because your luck is so bad. Maybe you'll start trying to compensate on the next putt for the way the last one missed—too high, too low, too short, or too long. You'll stop thinking of each putt as a unique entity and start correcting past mistakes on future putts. That's a form of getting in your own way.

I much prefer a player to react calmly to a missed putt—even two of them on the same green. Calmness says it doesn't matter if he missed that putt, because the player knows he's putting well and will soon hole some long ones to make up for the miss. Calmness says a player has too much confidence in his putting to get upset over a miss.

It may help to keep in mind that putting is not supposed to be easy and greens have been designed to make two-putts a challenging goal that no player will always meet. You're human. You're going to make mistakes. Golf is a game of mistakes, and that makes it a game that will beat you up mentally if you let it. You might as well have some compassion for yourself. From compassion comes forgiveness and from forgiveness comes forgetting. The only constructive thing you can do about a missed putt is to forget it. That way, you can be free and confident on the next one.

Your routine after making a putt isn't so problematic. It's fine to be happy if you hole one. Feeling the emotion helps cement the memory in your mind, and you want to remember your successful putts.

You can overdo it, of course. I don't see too many successful players who go bonkers when they hole a long birdie putt, even in a clutch situation. (I see some players, especially on the Senior tour, who do a pretty good imitation of someone going bonkers when they make a long putt, but I suspect these are people who consider it part of their job to entertain the galleries.) Most people who become good at golf have learned that it's best to maintain a low, consistent level of intensity through good shots and bad, because the calmer you are and the quieter you keep yourself, the easier it is to play the game.

Putting in the Clutch

Tension and anxiety cause more misses than lack of care.

—BOBBY JONES

LOTS OF PUTTS CAN BE CALLED CLUTCH PUTTS, BUT I CAN'T RECALL many that carried more pressure than a fifteen-footer that Cindy Figg-Currier faced on the last hole of the LPGA Qualifying School in October 1983.

Cindy, at that time, was just about a year out of the University of Texas. She'd grown up in Mount Pleasant, Michigan, and she'd been playing golf most of her life. Her father, who'd been a schoolteacher, had bought a little golf course called River-wood when Cindy was six weeks old. When she was a toddler, Cindy's toys were cut-down clubs with electrical tape for grips. The youngest of four kids, she hung around the putting green at Riverwood in the summer, chipping and putting against her older brothers and her sister. She learned the game by imitation, and she learned it the way kids should learn it, from the green back to the tee. By that I mean she learned to get the ball in the hole first, and only later worry about how to get it off the tee and up to the green.

Cindy was a good junior golfer in Michigan, but her swing was raw. When she got to Texas, the other women on the golf team nicknamed her "Trash Queen" because it seemed to them she was always beating them by getting her ball up and down from around the trash basket near the tee box on the next hole.

Harvey Penick, who worked a little bit with the Texas women, wisely saw this as an advantage for Cindy. He encouraged her to build on it, refining the way she hit her chips and pitches, teaching her how to handle different lies and grasses, when to bump and run and when to lob, how to play the wind.

When Cindy graduated from Texas, she had a degree in marketing and a decision to make. Should she get a job? Or should she follow her dream and try to make it on the LPGA Tour?

She decided to give professional golf a chance, but a limited one. She would take three shots at qualifying. But it would be three strikes and you're out. Or, in Cindy's case, three misses at qualifying school and she'd put up the clubs and try something else.

On her first try, in January 1983, she was not ready and failed. She came close on her second attempt, in August of 1983. But that was a vintage year for young women golfers. Among the players who made it through that qualifying school were Julie

Inkster and Rosie Jones. The LPGA recognized that some good players had been squeezed out, so it scheduled another school for October 1983. That would be Cindy's last chance.

The tournament was held at Sweetwater Country Club in Sugarland, Texas, where the LPGA then had its headquarters. Standing on the final tee, Cindy could see the scoreboard. She needed a birdie to qualify, and the 18th was a long par-4 with the approach over water. Cindy hit a good drive. Her second shot, a four-wood, cleared the water and landed on the green, stopping fifteen feet from the hole.

Now, you may think that a fifteen-footer on the 18th green to win a three-dollar bet from your buddies is a pressure putt. You may think that a fifteen-footer on the final hole to win a major championship is a pressure putt. You may agree with Lee Trevino, who once said that real pressure is putting for a hundred dollars when you only have ten in your pocket. But I think all of those pale next to Cindy's challenge—a fifteen-footer to determine the course of the rest of her life.

Her caddie that week was her older brother Marty. And as they walked across the bridge to the green, Marty had an inspiration that should earn him a spot some day in the Caddie Hall of Fame.

"I'll give you all the money I have in my pocket if you make that putt," Marty said.

Cindy smiled then. She still smiles now, telling the story. Marty's offer immediately transformed the emotional context of the putt. It was no longer a fifteen-footer that a young woman either had to make or start looking for a job. It was a game, just like all the games that a cocky kid sister had played with her older brothers on the putting green back in Mount Pleasant— delighting when she won, not caring all that much when she lost.

Cindy, of course, made the putt and got her LPGA Tour card. She still has it, and she's still a great clutch putter. Marty, as it turned out, had about fifty dollars in his pockets that day. Cindy used it to take him out to dinner that night in the Holiday Inn in Sugarland.

UNFORTUNATELY, THE MARTY Figg solution is not a universally applicable tool for taking pressure off putts. It was available only to Cindy, and even to her only once. She and the rest of us have to find another way to cope with putting under pressure, a way that can be used whenever we face a pressure putt, a way that will work time and again.

Fortunately, that way exists. And the power to use it is within you. It consists of developing a strong mental routine and relying on it in the clutch.

The cliché in discussions of pressure is to point out that pressure doesn't really exist. It's something that a golfer invents. After all, the two dollars you stand to lose if you miss that putt on the 18th green isn't going to affect your credit rating. If you miss the fifteen-footer to win the major, you're still going to make a nice check. Even in Cindy Figg-Currier's case, the worst outcome was that she'd have to do what all the rest of her class-mates had done, which was use her degree to make her way in the world. None of us is going to starve or die if we miss a putt. We're not going to lose our families, our houses, or anything else that's truly important if we miss the putt. It doesn't have to be important to us. Certainly the ball and the putter don't know whether the next shot is a ten-footer for a birdie to win a tour-nament or a ten-foot practice putt. And, as I sometimes tell players, a billion Chinese could care less whether their putts fall.

But so what? The fact is that we do care, we do put pressure on ourselves, and pressure can complicate the process of mak-ing a putt.

The professionals I work with face severe pressure, pressure so great it can make their hands shake. That's what happened to Jim Carter recently at the Tucson Open.

Jim was a relative latecomer to golf. He never played on a golf course until he was thirteen. He didn't start to play a lot until his family moved to Arizona a few years later. No one gave him a college golf scholarship. He went to Arizona State and tried to walk on to the team. He didn't make it originally, and he used to take his shag bag to an open field at Mesa Commu-nity College to practice, trying to get better. "I was behind my peers, and there's so much to learn about golf," he told me.

Jim was in his third year at Arizona State before he qualified for his first trip with the golf team. But once he got a chance to play, he improved rapidly. By his senior year, he won the

NCAA individual championship. He decided to give professional golf a try.

Jim was far from an immediate success. He felt as he had when he got to college, like a novice trying to catch up to peers who had years more experience than he did. He got his Tour card and lost it. He spent four years wandering in the wilderness of the minor league tours. He'd go to qualifying school each fall and terrible things would happen. Once he bogeyed the last four holes in a row and missed the cut by a shot. The next year he bogeyed two of the last three holes to miss by a shot again. "My confidence was shattered," he told me.

We worked on giving Jim a solid putting routine. Every time he putted, Jim tried to get behind the ball, make a brisk, decisive read, take his stance, take two looks at his target, and roll the putt. More important, he sought always to putt from that moment of clarity, that moment when he envisioned the way the ball would roll and believed firmly in it, when he thought of nothing else.

Jim got back to the Tour and stayed there. But over the course of five or so years, he couldn't win a tournament. He was making a living, but the Tour has its hierarchy, and there is a gulf between those who have won and those who haven't, a gulf that involves not just money, but pride and prestige. He wanted badly to win.

His chance finally came in Tucson. Jim led the tournament by two shots as he stood on the tee of the 72nd hole. He wasn't paying attention to the scoreboard, though. In fact, he thought his lead was only one, and that he'd need no worse than a par to stave off Steve Flesch and Len Mattiace, who were his closest pursuers.

The 18th hole in Tucson is a formidable challenge, a long par-4 where the tee shot must be long and straight, landing between two lakes. Then there's a long-iron approach shot and a tricky green. Jim handled the first two shots well, putting a three-iron into the fringe on the back of the green, perhaps twenty feet above the hole.

His situation seemed starkly clear. Get the ball in the hole in two shots and he'd do no worse than tie. Three-putt and the agonizing years of playing without a win would probably continue.

Fortunately, Jim had the sense not to think of the situation in those terms. He thought, instead, about his putting routine. He got behind the ball and found the line he thought it would take. He decided he wanted it to barely plop into the hole as its momentum died. He took two practice strokes to get the feel of the pace he wanted to give the ball. He stepped into his stance, took two looks at the target, and let the putt go.

It didn't go in, sliding by on the left side and stopping about two feet below the hole.

Now Jim felt his hands shaking. Adrenaline was coursing through his system. He felt, he told me later, as if he could have jumped nine feet into the air.

Instead, he relied again on his routine. He told his playing partners he would putt out. And he went through the process again—lining it up, forcing himself to focus on the path he expected the ball to take into the hole, achieving that moment of clarity. He took his practice strokes and took his stance. His hands felt as if they were going to fly off his arms. He took his two looks at the target and stroked the putt. It rolled straight into the center of the hole. Jim felt a rush of pride, relief—and joy. After all the years of struggle, he had finally broken through and won.

I cite this story because it dispels one of the common illusions about golfers who putt well under pressure. It's said that they have ice water in their veins, or they don't feel nervous. That's just media baloney. Great pressure putters have the same nerves, the same glands, and the same emotions that plague the twenty-handicap player in your foursome who always manages to blow the decisive three-footer. It's how they respond to nervous jitters that distinguishes them.

Their routines are the foundation of that response. As I've mentioned, golfers under pressure revert to their dominant habits. If your dominant habit is a routine that gets both your body and mind into position to putt well, you have a big advantage over players who haven't got a sound routine and find themselves trying to invent one in the clutch.

Part of this is physical. As Jim said to me after his Tucson win, going through the same movements he'd gone through uncounted thousands of times was soothing to him. It reminded him that the final putt in the Tucson Open was just a two-footer of the sort he'd made more often than he could remember. It reminded him of all the two-footers he'd made in practice. That's a good feeling to have under pressure. I tell players that they should make all their practice putts feel as if a tournament is on the line, and they should make all their putts with tournaments on the line feel like practice putts. Routine helps them do that.

But the larger part of it is mental. When a player who has a sound routine reverts to his or her dominant mental habit under pressure, it helps dispel distracting thoughts. It helps the player zero in on a target. That helps make the putt.

Dottie Pepper told me about one of the most satisfying putts she ever made, a putt that was critical to her first major championship. It was at the Dinah Shore tournament several years ago. Dottie was fighting it out with Julie Inkster for the title. They came to the final hole, which is a par-5. Dottie was a stroke behind. Julie missed her birdie putt, and Dottie faced a four-footer to force a play-off.

It was the sort of putt that can cause a major attack of nerves. Not too much break, but some. Close enough that you'd expect to make it, but not close enough to tap in. Close enough that you'd know, if you missed it, you'd blown a chance to break through and win a major.

Dottie was nervous, but she had long before determined that whenever she faced a pressure putt, she would rely on her routine. She did with this putt.

"By the time you get to that stage in a tournament, your feel for the greens is very instinctive," Dottie says. As she squatted behind the ball, she didn't have to work very hard to gauge the way it would break or the pace it needed. Her disciplined mind reverted to its dominant habit, striving for that moment of clarity, that feeling of decisiveness.

As it happened, a bug crawled onto the edge of the cup, right where Dottie intended to aim. Sluggishly, it stopped there. Some players would have been distracted, but Dottie wasn't. Her routine, her habitual search to find a target and focus on it, helped her. The bug simply reinforced the target line in Dottie's mind. She went through the rest of her routine aiming at the bug. She stroked the putt into the hole right over it. She won the first play-off hole and, with it, moved into the ranks of the LPGA's elite, its major championship winners.

GOOD PUTTERS LEARN to welcome nervous symptoms, rather than fear them. Nerves are something they don't feel during practice rounds. Nerves are something they feel when the stakes are high. Good players have practiced and competed for years precisely because they wanted to win tournaments where the stakes are high. So to them, nerves are a sign that their goal is approaching. They understand that nerves are a challenge, but they want to meet that challenge head-on.

Dana Quigley worked longer than most players to get to the point where he putted for a championship. Dana, like Jim Carter, was a latecomer to golf. Unlike Jim, he didn't have the advantage of growing up in a warm-weather state like Arizona.

Dana is from New England, where the golf season is pitilessly short. He started playing as a teenager in Rhode Island. He remembers trying out for his high school golf team as a sophomore and shooting 105.

Dana had a passion for golf, but he had other sports. He played basketball and ran track. Golf was a summer game, which he fit in between caddying jobs at the Rhode Island Country Club. He battled a tendency to slice the ball and he had no opportunity to take lessons. But he worked at the game when he could, imitating better players, especially his older brother, Paul. He improved. He made the high school golf team as a junior and by the time he was a senior, he could break 80.

That's nice, but merely shooting in the 70s won't attract hordes of college golf coaches to your door. Dana went to the University of Rhode Island and tried to walk on to the golf team. He didn't make it as a freshman. But he was persistent. He practiced whenever he could in a field by the college gym. Eventually, he made the team. But he never thought he was good enough to play on the Tour. He worked as a house painter and a club pro. He never won anything bigger than the Rhode Island Open. Finally one winter, on a lark, he entered the Tour's qualifying school. To his surprise, he made it.

He went out on the Tour with no confidence in his ability to compete. "I was scared to death of all the other players," he told me. "I drank and partied my way around for five years."

Dana managed to stay on the Tour that long because by that time he'd developed a reliable swing. He guesses that he aver-

aged 30–32 putts a round in those years, which will not win any
Tour events. He had a sense that he wasn't accomplishing anything. After five years he quit the Tour and went back to being
a club pro.

He had some bumps along the road. He got divorced. He
continued to drink. But in his forties, Dana started to pull himself together. He stopped drinking. He began to hone his game
again. He won a lot of regional events. As his fiftieth birthday
approached, he decided to give tournament golf another try.

He came to see me shortly before he started out trying to
qualify for Senior tour events. We worked a lot on his putting
routine, because we knew that on the Senior tour, putting is
perhaps even more critical than it is on the regular tour. Nearly
everyone at the senior level has a reliable swing, and the
courses are set up to make it relatively easy to hit and hold
greens. So putting becomes the decisive factor. We worked on
Dana's routine, particularly on the climactic part of the routine.
Dana had to learn to putt to make putts, not to avoid three-
putting, which is what he had tended to do for much of his golfing career.

Dana found early success on the senior tour. He qualified for
a tournament in Long Island on a Monday, then went out and
won the actual event. That earned him the right to play regularly on the Senior tour for a year. But it didn't solve all of his
problems with putting and attitude.

He still tended to see himself as slightly inferior to the players
who had been consistent winners on the regular tour. That was

especially true with his putting. He told me he understood that his peers on the Senior tour saw him as a good putter. He still had trouble seeing himself as a good putter, particularly under pressure.

But Dana is not the sort of man to back away from a challenge. That is a quality typical of good clutch putters. They not only don't back away from the challenge of putting under pressure, they've learned to love it. They love the fact that when they putt under pressure, their minds and bodies are totally engaged, totally committed. It's a feeling they don't get from driving a car or paying a mortgage or anything else in their lives.

Dana kept getting himself into position to win tournaments, into spots where his putts came with enormous pressure. Inevitably, that meant that if he wanted to win, he had to face down some players he'd all but idolized. Players like Tom Watson.

Watson charged hard at Dana in the final round of the TD Waterhouse Championship in Kansas City recently. Dana had had a wonderful tournament, shooting 65 and 67 in the first two rounds for a total of 132. But that wasn't enough to give him the lead. Going into the final day, Jim Colbert, with a 61 and a 69, for 130, was in front. Watson, with a 70–66, was in third. They all played together on the final day.

Dana took the lead for the first time on the back nine, when Colbert hit it in the water on 14. But Watson was playing a marvelous final round. He kept making birdies.

It was Watson's first professional tournament in his hometown, and the crowd of 25,000 was screaming its devotion to him. The ones who weren't pulling loudly for Watson were rooting for Colbert, who went to college at Kansas State. It was, Dana recalled later, like playing in the Ryder Cup—for the visiting team.

Playing the final hole, Dana had a one-stroke lead. He hit his approach to the green well, and got polite applause. Then it was Watson's turn. He hit an eight-iron that covered the flag. Dana couldn't immediately see where it stopped since the green was elevated. But the enormous roar told him Watson had knocked it close.

As he walked onto the green, the situation became clear. Dana was twelve feet away. But Watson was only a foot from the hole. He would have a tap-in birdie. Dana's challenge, then, was clear. He had to hole his own birdie putt or face Watson and the adoring hometown crowd in a play-off.

"You don't take pressure off a putt like that," Dana told me later. "You face it and deal with it."

Dana found out at that moment what his dominant habit was. He read the green and found the line he believed the ball would take. He took his stance and lined the putt up. It was, he figured, a putt that would break slightly from left to right. He settled on the left edge of the cup as his target.

And then he putted to make it. In the past, he might have putted not to three-putt, told himself to make sure he left it close, so that he could be certain of at least being in the play-off. That was how he had thought in the past. But thanks to all the work he'd put in on his putting routine, especially his mental routine, the dominant habit that emerged under pressure was the right one. He putted to make it.

Remember that when a player putts to make it, there is no past, nor is there a future. There is only the present moment, his ball, his club, and his target.

Had the past entered Dana's mind, he might have remembered how he'd fallen off the Tour when Watson was winning major championships. He might have thought about putts he'd missed. Had he thought about the future, he might have thought about a play-off, or the second place check, or any of a hundred other things that might happen. Those are the sorts of things players think about when they succumb to pressure. It's not that they choke. They don't. They simply let themselves be distracted by unhelpful thoughts of either the past or the future.

Dana's mind was firmly locked in the present. He stroked the putt. He remembers how firm and solid it felt. He remembers watching it track the line he'd foreseen, watching it drift a couple of inches to the right, remembers watching it fall into the hole.

Then he remembered all the times as a boy when he'd practiced putting, dreaming that the putt he was stroking was to make a birdie to take a championship from a great player. Finally, Dana thought, that dream had happened. It was a sweet feeling.

And that is how great players distinguish themselves on the green in clutch situations. They don't rely on tricks or gimmicks. They don't have superhuman control of their bodies. They don't avoid the churning stomach, the sweaty brow, the trembling hands. They simply do better than their competitors at enjoying the challenge, following their putting routines, locking their minds in the present, and putting to make it.

Speed:

The Light Is Always Green

The proper mental approach to a long putt is,
"I'm going to hole this one by making the ball
fall just over the front edge of the cup."

—CARY MIDDLECOFF

ONCE IN A WHILE, I WORK WITH A PLAYER WHO TELLS ME HE HAS NO touch. He rolls the ball way past the hole all the time. Or he leaves it way short. Or he hits it way past on one hole and then, compensating, he leaves it short on the next. Or he can't putt the fast greens at his best friend's club when he's invited for the member-guest. Or he can't adjust to slow, shaggy greens.

When someone tells me this, I usually respond by tossing them a ball. They catch it, and I ask them to toss it back. Without thinking about it, they toss it precisely into my hands.

"That's amazing," I say. "Your toss reached my hand exactly right. I didn't have to reach out for it. It didn't come in hard enough to sting me. I could just catch it."

The player nods, maybe grins a little.

Then I play the same game of toss-and-catch with an unfa-miliar object, like an ashtray or a stuffed animal. Instinctively, the player adjusts to the weight of the new object and tosses it the correct distance.

"That shows that you have good touch," I tell him. "Your problem isn't that you don't have touch. Your problem is that you're worrying about speed instead of putting to make it."

And that is true. The last thing you want to do if you're trying to make putts is worry about speed. Your brain, eyes, and ner-vous system are marvelously equipped to roll the ball at the right pace if you just let them respond naturally. All too often, though, golfers get in their own way on issues of speed. They decide that they don't have touch because they've left some critical putts short or rolled them too long.

Again, I find this kind of harsh self-evaluation both false and damaging, because the test wasn't fair. When I ask these play-ers what their mental state was when they made these speed mistakes, they almost invariably confess that they were putting fearfully, afraid of making a mistake with pace. Well, even the players with the best touch in the world are going to mishit putts when their minds are in that state. I simply ask players not to evaluate their touch until they have some experience putting with the proper attitude. And the proper attitude doesn't worry much about speed.

It's not that speed isn't important in making putts. It is. A player controls just two things when he putts a golf ball—line and pace. There are a few putts, the straight ones, where line is much more important than pace in determining whether the ball goes on the hole. But on breaking putts, the right line has to be married to the right speed. One doesn't work without the other.

If you don't understand this, try a little game that one of the best putters in the world, Brad Faxon, plays on the practice green. Brad takes three balls and finds a putt of about five feet with a moderate break. He then makes the putt at three differ-ent speeds. Hit firmly, the ball breaks very little, and the correct line is inside the hole. Hit at medium pace, the ball breaks more, and the correct line is perhaps a couple of inches outside the hole. Hit softly, the ball breaks quite a bit. Brad makes it plop over the side of the cup, dying into the hole.

If you try this game a few times, it will reinforce the knowl-edge that there is no uniquely correct line for most putts. Line is usually a function of speed, and vice versa. You'll start to see putts a little differently when you line them up. You'll be able to imagine several ways the ball might roll into the hole, and you'll begin selecting not only your line, but your speed.

But, the fact is that Brad Faxon, like nearly all the other good putters I know, never consciously thinks about speed when he's putting. He trusts his touch. When he reads a green and picks out a line, he's also thinking, subconsciously, of a speed that will make that line the correct one. When he strokes the ball, he's thinking about rolling it on the line he's selected, rolling it on the line that will take it into the hole. He lets the speed take care of itself. Nearly all the time, it does.

Now, I understand that Brad has some advantages over the typical amateur golfer. For one thing, he putts a lot. For another, the greens on the Tour tend toward a fairly consistent speed. They're almost always fast but not linoleum-fast. But I don't think Brad has innately better touch than most players. He's just more successful than most at trusting his touch. He tells me speed just happens.

I don't try to prescribe the appropriate speed for players. I know some, like Glen Day, who like to putt the ball so that it dies into the hole. I know others, like David Duval, who believe in hitting the back of the cup with most of their putts. Most players pick different speeds depending on the situation. They try to hit some putts firmly and others softly. There may be times when firmness is the smart option, such as a straight, up-hill three-footer on a green that's been spiked up. There may be times when a delicate touch is called for. I don't care what speed a player opts for as long as he's trying to put the ball in the hole.

THE PROPER PACE of a putted ball has engendered more myths and hogwash than almost anything else in golf.

Few people, I suspect, get through their first round of golf without hearing the adage "Never up, never in." It makes it seem as if the goal in putting is not to get the ball in the hole but to roll it past the hole. At least if you roll it past the hole, no one is going to call you "Alice" and question your boldness, your courage, your manhood.

I heard an interesting story about the origin of the "Nice try, Alice" remark that suggests how silly it is. According to this tale, the first time the words were uttered, the golfer was Peter Alliss, who's now a television commentator. He left a putt or two short in the British Open, and some fans sarcastically called out, "Nice try, Alliss." But by the time the words became common in American golf, they'd been subtly changed to "Nice try, Alice." Leaving a putt short had been transformed from simply a mistake to something effeminate. That made American golfers, who tend to be as macho as the next fellows, all the more determined to make sure they never left a putt short.

I'm sorry, but a miss is a miss—whether it runs a foot past the hole or stops a foot short. You get no extra credit for getting the ball past the hole. Good players understand this. They know that if they're trying to roll the ball in the hole softly, it's possible that it will stop a bit short of the hole. If it does, it's a mistake like any other. They go on.

The "never up, never in" concept, mistaken though it is, is nevertheless a model of lucid thinking in comparison to the notion of the green-light putt. The idea of the green-light putt, I suppose, is that this is a putt that the player can safely try to make. This implies that there are red-light putts, putts that are too fast, too slippery to try to make. What is the player supposed to do with them? Try to miss them?

The people who advance the notion that there are "green-light putts" and "red-light putts" tend to be, I find, people whose bad putting forced them into alternative careers as broadcasters. Giving them a microphone and encouraging them to talk about putting is a little bit like going to traffic court, taking all the people convicted of careless driving, and putting them in charge of driver education down at the local high school.

The truth is that every putt is a green-light putt.

That doesn't mean, of course, that you must hit the ball hard on every putt. Take the twenty-footer that Jim Carter had for his third shot on the final hole of the Tucson Open. It was a downhill putt and the green was fast. No sensible player would try to hit that putt hard enough so that the ball banged against the back of the cup as it went in. Obviously, in that case, a miss could roll ten feet past the hole.

But Jim nevertheless putted to make it. He simply tried to give it a pace to make sure that the ball was dying as it approached the hole. As it happened, he rolled it a couple of feet by.

In the course of a normal round, especially on fast greens, there are going to be some putts like that. When he faces them, a smart player may decide to hit his putt just hard enough to get it into the hole. If he does, he also reads more break into the putt, knowing that a slower putt will be affected more by the contour of the green. But he doesn't try to miss, doesn't say to himself, Where do I want to leave this ball for the next putt? He tries to putt the ball into the hole, just as much as he would for an uphill, four-foot par putt.

Occasionally, when I'm teaching amateurs, someone will hear this and say, "Well, that's fine for pros, Doc, but all I'm trying to do in that situation is avoid a three-putt."

Obviously, no one likes to three-putt. But putting to avoid

the three-putt is like trying very carefully to color inside the lines. It eliminates your artistry, your flair, your imagination. It also defeats your own purpose. When a child is told to try very hard to color inside the lines, she generally fails at it, because by trying too hard she robs herself of some of her fine motor skills. When a putter tries very hard not to three-putt, he generally winds up three-putting more often, and for similar reasons. He doesn't get the first putt on line, or he awkwardly leaves it too short or too long. And he will definitely make far fewer of his first putts.

I'm not suggesting that a golfer who putts every first putt to make it, whether it's uphill or downhill, fast or slow, will never three-putt. He will. All golfers do. But he will three-putt less often than the player who's afraid of three-putting. And he will one-putt more often. In the long run, he'll take fewer strokes.

SOME PLAYERS TELL me that their speed problems are not with fast or slow greens per se, but with making the transition from slow greens to fast, or vice versa. And there's no question that this kind of move requires an adjustment. If you're used to putting on shaggy, slow greens and you play a round on a course with fast greens, the stroke you applied to move the ball twenty feet on your regular course may move the ball thirty feet on the new course. Conversely, the stroke that had the ball rattling against the back of the cup on the fast greens of your home course can leave it short on a course with slow greens.

This can also be an issue from one day to the next in tournament play. The trend in setting up courses for tournaments these days is to make the greens as fast and firm as possible. Sometimes the grass is cut so short that it couldn't survive more than a day or so without being allowed to grow. If a course is hosting an event over several days, this means that the greens will likely get faster as the tournament goes on, with the superintendent waiting until the final day to mow them to their fastest possible speed. So tournament players have to be ready to adjust from one day to the next, even though they're on the same course.

Fortunately, the brain can do this for us automatically. You might find that you haven't got a feel for the proper pace on the first green you putt. But after that, your touch is going to get better. It will very quickly be as good as it was on your home course—as long as you keep your mind quiet and offer it no "instruction."

Still, some players don't like to wait for their brains to adjust, and there are a couple of things they can do to facilitate the adaptation. I don't have a problem with a player who gets to a new course early so he can spend some time on the practice green, rolling putts and getting a feel for their speed and the way they break. (Although, as I'll discuss further on, I don't think he should do this while putting to a hole.)

A player can also mentally shift his target backward or forward to help him compensate for a new and unfamiliar green speed. If the putt is downhill and fast, imagine a cup a foot or so short of the real cup, on the line you intend your ball to take.

Putt at that. Conversely, for slow, uphill putts, imagine a cup a foot or so behind your real target and putt at it.

This is not, I think, as effective as simply trusting your instincts and putting to your real target. If, however, you can't bring yourself to do that on a fast green, it's better than the alternative of putting fearfully, trying constantly to "fix" your perceived lack of touch. The best way to deal with speed is to remember that you already have touch. You just have to believe in it and use it.

The Yips

Some day you're going to realize how hard it is to make those putts. All you do now is aim and fire.

—SAM SNEAD, WHO HAD THE YIPS, TO BILLY CASPER, WHO NEVER GOT THEM

I WISH THERE WERE A WAY TO AVOID WRITING THIS CHAPTER. THIS IS a book about how good putters think. The yips are all about how bad putters think. I'm afraid that talking about the yips may be a bit like a high school coach telling his kids to steer clear of a roadhouse on the wrong side of the tracks. The coach may be putting ideas in impressionable minds that otherwise would never be there.

But I know that players do get the yips and want to get rid of them. It's been happening for a long time. The victims are quite often excellent players. In fact, they get the yips in part *because* they're excellent players.

Typically, what happens is this: A boy (yips seem to befall

men more often than women) learns to play the game in a natural way. His goal is simply to get the ball in the hole. He has a good short game, a confident approach to putting. He doesn't always hit the ball straight, but when he gets in trouble, he finds a way to score.

He starts to play golf well. He may start to win tournaments. Then someone says, "You've got a pretty funky swing there. Would you like to straighten it out, make yourself even better?"

The kid decides he would indeed like to perfect his golf swing. So he works at it, taking good advice, practicing long hours. And his swing gets better. By the time he's thirty-five or forty years old, he hits the ball a lot better than he did when he was twenty-two—maybe not quite as long, but a lot straighter. He hits fairways. He hits greens. From a kid who simply loved to play the game, he develops into a man who still loves it, but is a bit of a perfectionist about it.

But he doesn't win any more than he did when he was twenty-two, and it quickly becomes apparent to him why not. Improved ball striking doesn't necessarily lead to improved scoring. To improve his scoring, he has to improve his putting.

So he sets about improving his putting. He approaches it in much the same way he approached his long game. He works on improving his putting stroke. He gets obsessed with it. He's very conscious of things like whether his stroke is long and flowing, whether he keeps the putter blade square to the line, how the ball rolls after he hits it.

He's a perfectionist, and perfectionists are particularly susceptible to the yips. Perfectionists think they're simply setting high standards for themselves—and what's wrong with that? But the perfectionist carries it a step too far. No matter how well he putts, he's not satisfied. He remembers the one that missed instead of the ten or twenty that found the hole. It's not enough for him, in fact, that a putt goes down. It has to be center-cut. And if it isn't, the perfectionist berates himself, tells himself he's a lousy putter. Over time, he starts to believe it. And, as we've seen, people who think they're lousy putters generally become lousy putters.

So the player's putting gets worse. The player can't understand this. He keeps laying more and more pressure on himself to putt better. He starts to brood about the putts he misses, especially the short ones. And then, one day, something snaps. He takes his stance over a short putt. He can't draw the club back. Or, when he does, he can't smoothly stroke the ball. He has the yips.

One of the earliest recorded victims of this syndrome was the great Harry Vardon. By all accounts, Vardon was perhaps the best ball striker in golf history, at least until Ben Hogan came along. Using primitive clubs and balls, he was able to hit it where he wanted it to go with monotonous regularity. And for a number of years he must have been a great putter as well, because he won six British Opens back in the days when the British Open was essentially the only major championship for professionals.

"For many years, it did not so much as enter my head that I

could miss a short putt, except as the result of carelessness," Vardon wrote in his memoirs. "Then I struck a bad patch."

Vardon described this bad patch as the onset of a twitch that caused his right arm to jump and his grip to tighten. He felt helpless to solve the problem, though he recognized it was mostly mental.

"Once you lose your confidence near the hole, you are in a desperate plight," he said. "Especially if you have a reputation to uphold and you know that a putt of two feet counts for as much as the most difficult iron shot."

Vardon died, as far as I know, still suffering from the yips.

Sam Snead was able to pinpoint exactly when the yips struck him. It was late in 1946. Snead was then at the top of his game. He'd won the PGA, the British Open, and a slew of other tournaments. If there had been a world golf ranking system, he might have been first. Snead agreed to play a series of exhibition matches against Bobby Locke that winter in Locke's home country, South Africa.

Locke, who was probably the best putter of his era, gave Snead a humiliating beating on that tour, winning fourteen of the sixteen matches. Of course, he sank a lot of putts to do so. Snead wasn't able to shrug it off or attribute it to Locke's familiarity with the South African greens. He put more and more pressure on himself to match Locke's putting. Before the tour was over, Snead's stroke on short putts had deteriorated to an ugly, nervous jab. He had the yips.

Snead, who was then thirty-four years old, decided that as

middle age approached, something had gone wrong with his nervous system. He tried fixing almost everything about his putting game except the one thing that might have helped, his attitude. He switched putters; that seemed to help for a while. When switching putters no longer worked, he switched to a croquet style, with the putter drawn back between his legs. When the USGA banned that style, he changed to a style he called sidesaddle. And that was how he was putting when his tournament career ended. Snead was a great player, but there's no telling how much better he might have been if he hadn't developed the yips.

As the travails of Snead and Vardon show, the yips are hard to shake once a golfer has them. At an advanced stage, the golfer is so afraid of missing short putts that he all but freezes over the ball, fearful of what his hands will do when he tells them to move. When he finally does putt, his stroke is a jerky parody of his former movement, like one of those primitive silent films where the actors all look like they've got electrodes hidden in their bodies, making all their moves sudden and graceless.

A baseball player named Chuck Knoblauch developed a condition similar to the yips recently, and his symptoms suggest something about the nature of the malady. Knoblauch's problem was making the throw to first base. He got scatter-armed. On television one time, the broadcasters showed a replay of Knoblauch making a bad throw. He was actually looking at his throwing hand as he released the ball, rather than at his target, the first baseman's glove. He was that obsessed with the mechanics of releasing the ball. Putters with the yips, similarly, frequently get obsessed with physical factors like whether their left wrist breaks down during their stroke.

They do this despite the fact that there is no evidence I'm aware of suggesting the existence of a physical condition called the yips. Spasms, tics, and twitches are not an inevitable symptom of an aging nervous system, despite what victims like to imagine. The yips originate in the mind. Their prevention and cure are mental challenges.

The best solution for the yips is making sure you never get them in the first place. And you won't if you practice some of the mental disciplines we've already discussed in this book, disciplines that are integral to good putting.

Some of them have to do with your outlook toward putting. You must not forget that putting is a human endeavor and therefore will never be perfect. You are going to miss some putts, and some of those you miss will be so short they'll embarrass you. You may miss them because you misread them, or you had to putt over a lumpy green, or just because you mishit them. But you will miss them. You have to accept that fact— accept it as soon as each missed putt slides by the hole. Remember, that's part of a good routine.

Your memory can be either a bulwark against the yips or a fifth column in your golf game, subverting your confidence. If you dwell on the putts you miss, if you brood about them at night, you're more likely to develop the yips. If you forget your misses and develop the ability to remember your best putts, your attitude toward putting can get better and better as you age. Instead of developing the yips, you can be a calmer, steadier putter at sixty or seventy than you were at twenty or thirty. After all—who's made more putts, the twenty-year-old or the sixty-year-old? Who's got more great putts to remember?

Putters who develop the yips tend to be players who entertain ideas like, "You should make all your three-footers. . . . You can't afford to miss any par putts. . . ." They're skilled at finding ways to add pressure to the putts they face. They think this will force them to focus, force them to make putts. In reality, of course, it has the opposite effect.

Players who are immune to the yips tend to be players whose thoughts are less about results and more about process. The only thing they tell themselves they should or must do is follow their putting routine on each putt and love the joy of putting to make it. If they do that, they know they're going to hole the most putts they can possibly make. They're content with that.

Players who develop the yips tend to be players who don't understand that good putting is an uncontrolled, subconscious act. They want to guide or steer the ball into the hole. They try consciously to control their putting strokes, to make them perfect. When they stand over putts, they're not seeing the hole or seeing the ball go into the hole. They're seeing their hands, their putter blades, the line they want their blades to travel. They're trying to force their bodies to make their putters follow that path.

That sort of thinking—the conscious, forceful pursuit of putting perfection—overloads the mind and the nervous system the way turning on too many appliances can overload your house's circuit breakers. Something has to give. When it does, the yips are often the result.

Players who get the yips sometimes remind me of classically trained musicians who have been taught to believe that every note must be played exactly as the composer intended and try very diligently to do precisely that. Players who don't get the yips remind me of good jazz musicians, who may not even be able to read music, but who let the rhythm, the joy, and the creativity within themselves flow out when they perform.

The golfing equivalent of playing jazz is imagining the ball going into the hole and making a free, unconscious stroke—seeing it and doing it, as I sometimes tell players. You will never get the yips if you consistently just see it and do it.

Of course, not everyone can be this way all of the time. Even good putters have days when their minds are less clear and less quiet and their strokes are more tentative. They can't quite bring themselves to simply see it and do it. On such days, a good putter might experience a pang of doubt, a prickling feeling of fear. He might, indeed, see the ball missing the hole instead of dropping in. When he does, though, a good putter catches himself. He doesn't allow one mental mistake to build on another. He reverses the negative tendency in his thinking and becomes more casual, less controlled, more reactive. He doesn't allow a pang of doubt to become a full-blown case of the yips, any more than a person who takes care of his health would permit a head cold to develop into pneumonia.

SO WHAT IF you already have the yips?

I'm sorry to tell you that you can't practice your way out of them. If three-foot putts are your nemesis, you can spend twelve hours a day, seven days a week on the practice green sinking three-foot putts. But no matter how much you practice, if you don't change your attitude, the next time you face a three-footer that really matters to you, you're likely to see the yips return.

It's a little bit like what happened to a catcher named Mackey Sasser for the New York Mets a few years back. Mackey had a yiplike problem throwing the ball back to the pitcher with men on base. He'd pump, pump, pump—but he couldn't pull the trigger, couldn't just take the ball out of his glove and toss it back. It didn't matter how often Mackey practiced throwing the ball back to the pitcher in between games. His problem wasn't that he didn't know how to throw it back, after all. His problem was that he couldn't bring himself to do it in certain situations. So practicing the mechanics didn't help Mackey with his yips and they won't help you with yours.

There are some short-term cures that people have tried. Some players switch putters. Some change their grips. Some go to the long putter. Quite often, these changes bring some temporary relief, as we saw in the case of Sam Snead. That relief usually lasts as long as it takes for the player to begin applying his analytic mind to the question of *why* the new grip, new stroke, or new putter works better than his old way. As soon as he does that, he's applying his conscious mind to the problem of putting the ball in the hole. And when that happens, he's on his way to developing a renewed case of the yips.

But it's not hopeless. It's not true, as someone once said, that once you've had the yips, you've always got them.

The only sure cure is a difficult one. The player has to go back to the mental fundamentals of good putting. He is in a position somewhat analogous to a carpenter who's built a house that just doesn't work. Rather than keep adding joists and beams and buttresses in an effort to make it work, he's got to tear it down and rebuild from the basement up.

For a putter, this means rediscovering a carefree, cocky attitude about putting. It means not caring if you miss a short putt or two, because you know you're a good putter and you'll make up for it down the line. It may mean developing a sense of humor about putting, cultivating the ability to laugh at your own mistakes. It means developing the capacity to accept error and go on. It means developing a short memory for your misses and a long memory for your successes. It means giving up the illusory quest for the perfect stroke. It means committing yourself to a routine that includes seeing the ball going to your target and stroking the ball unconsciously.

If you attend professional golf tournaments, it might help you to follow a good putter for a couple of rounds and notice how often he misses a short putt. It will happen. Then see if you can detect any reaction to that miss beyond a wince or a groan as it slides by. Does the player's routine change on subsequent putts? Does his body language change? Does he start growling at his caddie? I suspect that the answers to all of these questions will be no. Otherwise, the player wouldn't be a good putter. Your reaction to missed putts should be similar.

It's much easier, I know, to write these things than it is to live them. If you have the yips now, you're not going to find it easy to reconstruct your entire mental approach to putting. But that is the only cure. If you can do it, you'll gradually become more confident about your putting, until finally someone in your foursome will remark how solid you are on short putts. And then someone else will say, "Didn't you once have the yips?"

And you'll have to pause for a moment to remember that, yes, you did once have them, just as you had mumps, chicken pox, and other ailments that you've long since forgotten.

New Putters, New Grips,
Old Problems

*A putter is like a woman. Treat it with care
and it will treat you right.*

—Gene Sarazen

Gene Sarazen, the first golfer to complete the modern career slam, told the best story about a putter I've ever heard. The year was 1932. Sarazen had a blade putter similar to the one that Bobby Jones had used and called Calamity Jane. Sarazen had customized his version by sawing it off at the neck and welding the blade to the hosel so that it had a bit more loft. (These were the days before the equipment manufacturers followed the Tour in mobile workshops staffed by specialists who work with the pros' clubs. Professional golfers of Sarazen's generation knew how to do this for themselves.) Maybe he should have called it Calamity Gene.

Sarazen took the putter to England with him for the British

Open on the prince's course in Sandwich, adjacent to Royal St. George's. Sarazen played brilliantly in that Open, winning by five shots. His 283 set a scoring record that stood for eighteen years, till Bobby Locke broke it in 1950 at Troon.

In those years, the British Open was played before the U.S. Open each summer, and when Sarazen came home, he still had his own national championship to look forward to. He did something many would think peculiar. He put his favorite putter in a locker and left it there for a few weeks. He pulled it out of the locker just before the U.S. Open began.

Once again, Sarazen was brilliant. Playing at Fresh Meadows Country Club in Flushing, New York, he covered the last 28 holes of the tournament in 100 strokes and won with a 286, tying the Open scoring record.

Why had he put his favorite putter in a locker between tournaments? Sarazen explained it some years later. He knew that he usually need some time to adjust from British greens to American greens or vice versa. He knew that he would miss some putts while he was making that transition. He didn't want to lose faith in his trusty putter. So he put it away and let some lesser club take the blame for the misses he knew he could expect. When he put Calamity Gene back in his bag, it was, to his mind at least, unsullied. And, not coincidentally, he won with it.

Sarazen's little putter ploy worked because it respected one of the psychological rules of putting: If you think the putter you're using will help you, it probably will. Conversely, if you think the putter you're using is worthless, it most likely will be.

The truth, if we define truth objectively, is that it shouldn't matter much which putter a player uses. A good putter can get the ball in the hole with an old shoe if he has to. And any putter you pick up, unless it's been sloppily built or damaged, is going to be a much better instrument for rolling a ball than an old shoe. Its grip, its shaft, and its blade have all been designed to facilitate putting a straight stroke on the ball and making it roll into the hole.

Most of the best putters I know long ago found a putter they liked. Years later, they're still playing with it, or something very similar to it. In fact, I've seen players get quite disconcerted if they sign an endorsement deal with a new equipment company and try to play that company's putter. Even if the new club is essentially the same kind of putter as their old favorite, they're unable to believe in it. Once in a while, you even see someone painting over the brand name on the old putter so that it won't show on television and no one will wonder why he's got a putter from Company A when his bag says Company B, or vice versa.

But I've also known players whose putting responded very well to a change in clubs or a change in grip. And I have been around golf long enough to have a healthy respect for whatever works. I would not have told Gene Sarazen he was deluding himself to think it made a difference to put his British Open putter in storage for a month. I don't tell a modern player who starts sinking putts after changing clubs that he's being foolish.

My primary concern is that a player stand over the ball knowing she's going to make her putt. It pleases me if she came by that confidence by thinking the problem through and adopting a sound mental putting routine. But if her confidence stems from the fact that she dreamed the previous night that her putter had been blessed by the Good Putting Fairy, it's likely to serve her just as well—at least until someone convinces her that fairies don't exist.

I'VE MENTIONED HOW Paul Azinger has worked to develop a mental putting routine that enables him to feel as free and unconscious and target-oriented with his putting as he has always felt with his sand game. One day, in the midst of that process, he happened to be in a pro shop and he saw one of the long-shafted putters, the kind that a player manipulates by sticking the butt end into his body around his sternum and making a pendulum stroke, moving the club with his right hand. It's a club that a lot of players go to when they have lower back problems, because they don't have to bend over to use it and they can, consequently, practice longer with it.

Paul picked up the long club and casually tried it on the floor of the shop. He immediately felt that his putting stroke got longer, more graceful and rhythmic, more natural, more free. He soon started using the long putter in competition, and he was using it when he won the Hawaiian Open, his first Tour victory since his battle with cancer.

Did the long putter help him? Well, I know his putting got

better. I think the more important factor, by far, was the effort Paul was making to get freer with his stroke, to gain control by giving up control. But maybe the switch to the long putter helped him make the mental transition from a feeling that he was forcing his stroke to a feeling that he was simply seeing it and doing it.

In a similar way, I've seen players get good results from switching putting styles, especially by going to the left-hand low, or cross-handed grip. I don't think this is because cross-handed is mechanically superior to the more traditional grip. I think it's because players who try it find that the new grip allows them to putt confidently, freely. They assume that the new grip will prevent a recurrence of the stroke problems they believe have been plaguing them. They start to see it and do it.

Unfortunately, this confidence usually lasts only until they miss a few putts they feel they should have made. At that point, they react by analyzing what went wrong with the new grip, why it failed. At about that time, some teacher or magazine article might "enlighten" them about some of the technical flaws in the cross-handed grip. The players fall back into the same pattern of thought that soured their putting with the old grip. Quite often, they start wondering as they putt which grip they ought to be using.

I don't know anyone who putts well when his mind is occupied by doubts about his grip.

That's why, if a young player asked my advice about putters and grips, I would advise him to pick a putter and a putting style that felt good to him and stick with them. Putting, after all, isn't about which club is best or which grip is best. It's about whose mind can best master the discipline that putting requires.

A player who gets hung up on putters and grips reminds me of an actor who says he can't get into his role as Hamlet because he doesn't like the skull he's been given as a prop for his "To be or not to be" soliloquy. I'd tell him that good actors don't care about their props. They're too busy looking within themselves for the emotions that will make their performance alive and real. In the same way, the golfer obsessed with his putter or his grip is focusing on the props and not on the core of his performance.

The Myth of the Perfect Stroke
and the Perfect Roll

*The fact is that a ball struck with a putter in
anything like a normal way will have no spin
at all. The contact is not brisk enough to
cause the ball to do anything but roll.*

—BOBBY JONES

WHAT I AM ABOUT TO SAY WILL BE AS POPULAR IN SOME QUARTERS AS
an assertion that Earth has never been visited by extraterrestrial
beings and there are no white alligators in the New York City
sewer system. Even though the evidence would support my
statement, there are a lot of people who would prefer to think
otherwise.

But I'll come out and say it anyway. There is no such thing as
perfect putting mechanics. There is no perfect way to roll the
ball.

In fact, there are any number of putting strokes and styles
and they can all work, depending on the mind of the player
who employs them. And a golf ball is designed to roll pretty

much the same way no matter how you stroke it. The stories you may have heard or read about the perfect stroke or about "hole-hunting spin" are golf's equivalent of tales about UFOs and albino alligators.

A lot of people believe them, and some of these people are good putters. But in my judgment they're good putters despite believing in those things. They're good putters because they believe in their method and because at the moment of truth, they're not distracted by thoughts of a perfect stroke or a perfect roll. They're focused exclusively on the target.

More typically, golfers get in their own way with thoughts about their stroke or the way the ball rolls. A rabbit could hop out of the hole in the middle of their putting routine and they wouldn't notice. They'd be too busy thinking about taking the clubhead straight up and down the line or putting overspin on the ball to be conscious of the target. And I don't know anyone who lets stroke mechanics or the roll of the ball dominate his mind that way and still putts well.

If you're a player who believes in perfect roll, try this experiment. The next time you're out at your golf course, take a striped range ball over to the practice green. Squat down about twenty feet away from a hole. Roll the ball toward the hole using your hand instead of a club. Try to give it the most violent sidespin you can, like a baseball pitcher throwing a curve ball.

The stripe will allow you to see the ball's spin better than you could with a normal ball. What you'll see is that the sidespin lasts for a few feet at most. Then it dissipates. The ball rolls end over end, as it were. It has topspin.

Then try it with a putter. Hit the ball toward the hole, putting as much sidespin on as you can. You will find that you can't put nearly as much sidespin on the ball with your putter as you could with your fingers. The spin you can put on the ball is infinitesimal. You probably won't even be able to see it.

So what would happen if you were trying to hit the ball straight, with no sidespin?

Right. Sidespin would play no role at all in how the normal putt behaved.

The fact is that the ball is round and it's going to roll in the direction you hit it. High-speed video of golfers' putting strokes confirms this. The films show that sidespin dissipates so quickly that it's basically irrelevant in determining where the ball goes on putts of more than a foot or so. They show that you don't have to worry about overspin. The laws of physics will give the ball overspin if you just hit it toward your target.

I know that some great players of the past, like Locke and Vardon, claimed they could cut or hook putts. Maybe with the lofted putters of their day they could in fact put a little sidespin on the ball. (More likely, they were simply describing what they perceived as the ball curved.) But the evidence is that today's putters on today's greens cannot put any significant sidespin on the ball.

Nor is there any evidence I've seen to support the proposition that a certain kind of spin helps the ball fall in the hole. Speed can help determine whether a putt goes in. A ball rolling slowly is more likely to drop along the edges of the hole than a ball rolling quickly. But by the time the ball reaches the hole on a putt, it's going to be rolling in the direction you hit it, modified by the break of the green. It can't do anything else. Speed and line are the only factors at work in deciding whether it falls.

If, despite this, a golfer stands over a putt and thinks, I want to put overspin on this ball, he's doing two things. First, he's trying to do something entirely superfluous. It's as if the pilot of a jet plane thinks, I know that planes make a lot of noise when they take off, so I'd better make sure this one does. Then he opens the cockpit window and roars like a lion as the plane taxis down the runway. He doesn't need to do that. If he's got the engines running properly, the airplane will make more than enough noise.

Second, and more important, the golfer who's thinking about overspin isn't thinking about his target, any more than the roaring pilot is thinking about his flight plan. He's liable to jab at the ball with an upward, wristy motion, trying to impart overspin. He's going to make fewer putts than he should.

Hey, it's a ball. Balls roll.

IF YOU BELIEVE in perfect putting mechanics, I invite you to think back to one of the most dramatically successful putts in recent golf history, the one from about forty feet that Justin Leonard sank on no. 17 at The Country Club in Brookline to win the 1999 Ryder Cup for the United States.

If you looked at Justin Leonard and believed what you'd read about putting mechanics, then you'd have to conclude that his putt was some kind of mass delusion shared by the American team, the European team, and forty thousand screaming spectators. Because, based on every theory of putting mechanics I've ever heard of, Justin could in no way sink that putt.

Experts on putting mechanics say you have to stand with your eyes directly over the ball in order to see the line properly and stroke the putt along that line. Justin's stance leaves his eyes well inside the target line. The experts say a putter's arms should hang straight down from his shoulders to promote a pendulum stroke. Justin putts with his arms extended away from his body.

How could he hope to sink that putt with such grievously flawed mechanics?

The answer, obviously, is that there's more than one acceptable way to stroke a putt. What matters is where the player's mind is as he strokes it. And I am sure that when he stood over that ball, Justin was thinking only of getting it into the hole.

I'm not suggesting that you adopt Justin Leonard's stance and stroke, or anyone else's for that matter. I am suggesting that your present stance and stroke are probably a lot more effective than you've been led to believe—if your mind is in the right place when you use them.

Golfers today are inundated with information and pseudo-information about the mechanics of putting. The implication in much of it is that a perfect stroke exists and that if you could only attain it, you would putt perfectly. Golfers put stock in this information, I think, because it's more comfortable to believe that their stroke is flawed than that their mind is weak. A flawed stroke, after all, is something that can be blamed on bad instruction or bad coordination. A flawed mental approach edges uncomfortably close to a character issue in some players' minds.

So we have many players in hot pursuit of the perfect putting stroke. The more putts they miss, the more convinced they become that their stroke is to blame. The more information they get about the stroke, the more lost they become in thoughts of mechanics. The more lost they become, the worse they putt. And so it goes.

Let's remember that when we're talking about putting, we're talking about something considerably simpler on a mechanical level than, say, riding a bicycle. Suppose we devised a new athletic event, the suburban biathlon. It would comprise a one-mile bicycle ride to a golf course, followed by a putting contest. During the bike portion of the event, the mechanics would be indeed complex. Contestants would have to steer, balance themselves on two thin wheels, pedal, brake, shift gears, and watch out for traffic—simultaneously! Yet I'd bet that nine out of ten of them would do most of these things subconsciously and naturally, simply keeping their eyes on the road ahead.

These same people, though, would probably turn very conscious and deliberate when they got off their bikes and had to putt. Yet putting a ball along the ground is so much simpler and easier physically than riding a bike. People already know how to do it. They don't have to think about it.

The irony is that the contestants most likely to turn conscious and deliberate when they started to putt would be the experienced golfers. That's because of all the information they've ingested about the putting stroke. That's because of the ethos in the golf world that worships mechanical perfection. There's a strong socialization process at work and it leads to conscious, unsuccessful putting.

You will hear quite often, for instance, that moving the head while you putt is deadly. Yet I remember an incident several years ago at the Walt Disney Tournament. I was working on the practice green with Brad Faxon. A teaching pro Brad knew was standing nearby, having come down to Florida to watch the tournament. This teaching pro had his video camera out, and he noticed Ben Crenshaw practicing near Brad. He prevailed on Brad to invite him inside the ropes. Then he prevailed on Crenshaw to let him tape Crenshaw's practice.

After one of Crenshaw's typically elegant strokes, the teaching pro asked, "What are you working on, Ben?"

"I'm trying to make sure my stroke feels long to short and really leisurely and my head moves a little bit."

In a single, two-second sentence, Crenshaw had contradicted all of the conventional wisdom this pro had learned about putting.

"Because every time I start putting badly, my stroke gets stiff and feels really short to long and, man, I never have any rhythm or flow when I feel like that," Crenshaw replied. "So I'm just trying to get my head moving and my stroke just leisurely going through it."

The teaching pro lowered his video camera, stunned. I have sometimes wondered whether he went home and continued to tell his pupils that the secret to putting well was a short-to-long, accelerating stroke with a still head, or whether he began teaching the opposite. I suspect that he made a valiant effort to suppress what he'd heard and keep on teaching conventional putting mechanics. As I said, there's a strong socialization process at work here.

I am not, in recounting this story, suggesting any particular stroke or head movement. In fact, it's conceivable that Crenshaw was telling the teaching pro what his stroke felt like to him on that day, rather than describing what he was actually doing. Golfers are frequently less than accurate in the way they perceive their own movements.

But the story does illustrate how one of the game's best putters, when he thinks about mechanics, thinks about contradicting so much of what everyone "knows" about putting.

The idea that there is a single correct way to putt is about as valid as the idea that there is a single correct way to write. Where would we be if all of us were told that the only way to write was to copy Shakespeare? We would be without a host of great writers, from Mark Twain to e.e. cummings. The same goes for putting mechanics.

This is why some of the great putters I know make a conscious effort not to think about mechanics at all when they practice. I've seen people ask Brad what part of the stroke he's working on when he practices.

"Nothing," Brad replies.

"Oh, come on," they say. "You must be working on something."

"I am," he says. "I'm working on thinking about nothing mechanical."

IN FACT, THE worst way to try to make a great stroke is by thinking about its mechanics when you putt the ball. As we've seen, the physical work of putting is like riding a bicycle or signing your checks. It's something best left to your subconscious. If you consciously try to guide your putter along a path you've been taught is the correct one, you're reducing the chances that you'll make a smooth, solid, accurate stroke. That's the way the human body works.

On the other hand, if you allow your brain and the nervous system to perform at their best, without interference from your conscious mind, they can do some remarkable things. I know players who have always aimed a little bit left of their targets. They didn't think they were doing it, but they were. However, they didn't hit all their putts left of the hole. As long as they were target-oriented, their brains subconsciously adjusted and altered their strokes enough to send the ball where they wanted it to go.

It's only when such players become conscious and rational about their strokes that they get into trouble. If a player who aims left makes it his business to force the putter to go straight up and down the target line, he's going to miss left. He'll be overriding his subconscious mind's ability to make the adjustment that would have sent the ball toward the target.

If you want to have a flowing, rhythmic, and elegant putting stroke, the last thing to do is think about flow, rhythm, and elegance when you're putting. That will make your stroke tight and strained, more like a jab at the ball. If, on the other hand, you're properly focused on your target, your body will naturally produce the most rhythmic, elegant stroke it can make. I know this because of what I see and hear around Tour practice greens. When a player I'm working with is sharply focused on his target, I can see that his stroke is smooth and flowing. I can tell by what I hear from other players, caddies, and swing teachers that I am not the only one who sees this.

If, after reading this, you nevertheless feel your putting stroke needs work, try this: Go to the practice green and try to make some four-foot putts, the kind that you're probably missing on the golf course. If you can make the four-footers on the practice green but not on the course, then your problem isn't your stroke. If you can't make the four-footers on the practice green, then maybe your mechanics do need work. If so, there are a few things you can do to help prevent your stroke-improvement effort from undermining your putting.

First, go to a good teacher and take a lesson in putting mechanics. Determine the fundamentals you plan to incorporate into your putting game. Commit yourself to staying with them. This means that for the foreseeable future, you are going to putt with the grip, the stance, and the posture you and your teacher agreed on. Players who are constantly fiddling with new grips and postures in an effort to find the perfect stroke can almost never free themselves of mechanical thoughts when they're in competition. Settle on a physical method and stick to it.

Second, practice it off the golf course. I'll talk more in a subsequent chapter about ways to do this. For now, suffice it to say that when you're on a putting green, putting at a hole, you want to be completely focused on getting the ball into that hole. This applies particularly to amateurs whose practice time is limited. A pro might get away with spending an hour on the practice green working on his stroke, because he has an additional hour and fifteen minutes to work on getting the ball into the hole. The amateur rarely has so much time.

Third, don't forget that putting remains more an art than a science. If you immerse yourself in the so-called science of putting, you risk filling your mind with ideas of dubious value (and dubious scientific validity). You risk losing the attitude and habits of mind that characterize great putters.

Imitation of other players can be a better way of improving your stroke. I have clients on the tour who spend time on the practice green pretending they're Ernie Els or Brad Faxon. They think their stroke needs a little of Ernie's and Brad's languid flow. So they imitate them.

This mimics the natural process that kids go through when they pick up a game by watching older people do it. It bypasses all the lectures about mechanics that usually accompany putting lessons and therefore it poses less danger to your mental putting routine.

But if any of the great majority of golfers asked me what I thought they should do about their putting stroke, I'd tell them this: Fall in love with the stroke you have. It's more than good enough to get the ball into the hole.

Practice to Get Better

Around the greens, my father tells me, I was deadly. But, then, I had spent so much time practicing.

—BOBBY LOCKE, SPEAKING OF HIS YOUTH

MY FRIEND AND CLIENT BILL SHEAN HAD A ROUGH TIME ON THE greens during the qualifying rounds of the most recent U.S. Senior Amateur Championship. Bill is a crackerjack senior golfer. In 1998, he won the U.S. Senior Amateur in his first year of eligibility. Nine months later he won the 1999 British Senior Amateur. Not many golfers have simultaneously held British and American national titles. The list includes Tiger Woods, Lee Trevino, Ben Hogan, Bobby Jones, and a few others—not bad company for a guy who sells insurance for a living and plays little or no golf from November to April each year.

To reach the elite level in senior amateur competition, Bill had worked particularly hard on his putting. He reasoned, correctly, that the higher one goes in tournament competition, the more the ball-striking differences among the players diminish and the more putting becomes decisive. He had not thought of himself as a particularly good putter when he was in his early fifties. By the time he reached fifty-five, the age of eligibility for senior amateur tournaments, he had made himself into an excellent one.

But at this championship, the greens were giving Bill trouble. The tournament was held at the Charlotte Country Club in North Carolina, an old Donald Ross layout that had been reworked by Robert Trent Jones. The greens were deep and narrow, with plenty of swales and tiers. And during the early part of the tournament, they were still wet from several days of rain.

Wet greens can be harder to figure than dry ones. Greens don't hold moisture equally over their entire surface. Some areas, because of drainage and exposure to the sun, dry faster than others. That may have been why Bill misjudged a couple of putts badly early in the first round, rolling them eight or ten feet past the hole.

The ensuing three-putts unnerved him. He took forty putts in the first round and forty more in the second round, which was played on a Tuesday morning. He was surprised when his two-round total of 157 made the field of sixty-four golfers for match play. He was barely under the cut line.

Because of the rain delays, there was no overnight break between the end of the qualifying rounds and the first round of match play. Bill had three hours before his first round match. He decided to use that time to practice in an effort to regain confidence in his touch, his ability to judge the pace on the tournament greens.

But Bill did not, as many golfers would, spend those three hours putting several balls to a distant hole on the green. Bill is a golfer who has thought a great deal about how to practice effectively. He knows that one of the guiding principles of effective practice is that you don't putt balls to holes so far away that you can't make the vast majority of the putts you try.

So Bill did what I would recommend to anyone who wants to practice to sharpen his sense of pace, his touch. He putted to the edge of the practice green.

He did this very deliberately. He took a few balls onto the green. He selected lines that offered some complications—sideslopes, downhill, uphill. He putted a single ball along each line he selected. He went through the core of his routine with each one. His goal was to make each ball stop precisely on the border between the green and the fringe. As time passed, his putts started to do so more and more often. Gradually, he rebuilt his confidence in his touch.

When match play began, Bill's putting was transformed. He sank three birdie putts during the early holes, from distances of six to fifteen feet. He felt that he had the ball once again under control—that it would go not only on the line he wanted but the distance he wanted. He started winning matches. Despite having barely made it through qualifying, Bill went all the way to his second U.S. Senior Amateur championship, putting well the entire time.

I TELL THIS story because I think it highlights a few important principles about putting and putting practice.

First, I don't think Bill had to "learn" the speed of the greens at Charlotte Country Club by practicing for three hours. He's an experienced tournament player with a number of USGA events under his belt. He knows how to putt on fast greens. And, as I've said, golfers have already got touch. What they sometimes lack is confidence in their touch. Bill had lost his confidence because he allowed some missed putts early in the event to bother him.

Nor do I think that hours and hours of putting practice are necessary to become a good putter or to maintain your skills. On the contrary, the most important factor in putting well is the confidence that enables the player to see it and do it, simply and subconsciously. Some players can see it and do it the moment they step onto a putting green. They don't need to practice much at all. That's fine with me. But other players either generally or on certain occasions need to practice before they can feel that confidence. Bill Shean is like that. And that's fine, too.

Basically, all that matters is that when you putt in competition, you putt freely and with confidence, seeing your target and letting the stroke go. If you can get to that point with little or no practice, fine. Use the time you save to work on other parts of your game. But if you're the sort of player who builds confidence through practice, do as Bill did. Practice wisely. Practice in ways that build confidence. Practice in ways that reinforce and strengthen your mental routine.

If you practice putting correctly, it should help your game. But I see a lot of golfers, particularly amateurs, who spend a fair amount of time on the practice green and then complain that their putting isn't getting better. They go on to conclude that they just don't have any talent for it, and they give up on becoming good putters. What's really happening is that they're practicing the wrong way. And if you do that, you can get worse.

There are no universally applicable drills or practice programs that will help all players. Just as individuals respond best to different putting stances and grips, individuals need different practice regimens. You have to be your own coach in this regard. You have to experiment a little with different drills and practice routines and find the ones that help your confidence, that help you get ready to putt to make every putt.

I have, however, observed a lot of practice regimens. I think there are a few guidelines that will help most, if not all, putters.

First and foremost, when you practice with a ball and a hole, always putt to make it. This isn't easy to do if you're twenty feet away from the hole and have several balls in front of you. It's very hard in those circumstances to avoid the tendency to get sloppy with your mental routine, to be content with simply rolling balls in the general direction of the hole.

Consequently, a lot of the good players I've seen and worked with emphasize short putts in their practice routines. When David Duval practices putting, he works most of the time from two to six feet. He's not the only one. You might think that putters of David's caliber would practice from longer range because, after all, they're already very good at shorter putts.

But they continually practice short putts, for a number of reasons. Practicing from close range assures them of making most of the putts they try. There's nothing better for your confidence and your putting than seeing balls go in the hole time after time. Second, they know the critical importance of short putts. If you're solid from, say, two to five feet, it makes it so much easier to make your longer putts. You can stroke them more confidently when you know that if by some misfortune you do miss, you're a cinch to sink the next one. Putts in the range of roughly five feet to seven feet are critical because they occur most often in two situations—when a player has hit his approach shot very well and has a chance to make birdie, and when he's missed the green, knocked a chip or pitch fairly close, and needs to save par. Good players will tell you that the difference between low rounds and high ones is usually sinking short birdie putts and getting up and down to save par when they miss greens. To me, short putts are the golfing equivalent of basketball's lay-up shot. The short putt, like the lay-up, is the foundation skill upon which all else is built. It's no coincidence that basketball teams get ready for every game by practicing lay-ups. It's equally true that good golfers make sure their short-putting skills are always honed.

Some players have short putting drills they perform as faithfully each day as brushing their teeth. Dottie Pepper, for example, takes three balls to the practice green and finds a reasonably straight putt to a particular hole. Then she sticks tees in the ground three feet, five feet and seven feet from the hole. She putts till she makes three in a row from three feet. Then she places the balls five feet away and tries to make all three of them. If she misses one, she starts over at three feet. And she keeps on this way until she's made nine putts in a row—three from three feet, three from five feet, and three from seven feet. Some days this takes her ten minutes. Some days it takes an hour. No matter how long it takes, she does it.

The drill does several things for Dottie. First, it enables her to see a lot of putts falling. Even if she doesn't complete the drill on the first try or two, she's going to make the vast majority of the putts she attempts. Second, it makes her feel that her putting is reliable and consistent from seven feet in. Third, it simulates putting under tournament pressure. If you don't believe this, try the drill. If you fail to complete it a few times, and then make eight in a row, I guarantee you're going to feel a little pressure on the ninth putt.

This last element suits Dottie. She likes the feeling of pressure while she practices. It helps her to be calm and free on the golf course. When she steps up to a critical short putt, she feels, This is easy. I did it nine times in a row in practice yesterday.

Other players tell me they don't feel that way. They find that when they're on the course, the memory of practicing under pressure only adds to the pressure they feel with actual putts.

They think, You can't miss this. You'll have wasted all that practice time.

Only a player can judge whether he's like Dottie or not. If you aren't, and you'd prefer to practice without that much pressure, there are other ways to do it. You could simply putt from, say, two, four, and six feet, until you'd made a specified number of each length. Misses wouldn't count. Stewart Cink likes a drill where he places tees in a circle around the cup, mimicking the face of a clock with a diameter of, say, three feet. Then he sinks a putt from every tee.

The main thing is that when you putt with a ball and a hole, you're putting to make every putt and you're making all or nearly all of them.

That's why I think practicing for touch and pace is best done without a hole. When you practice for touch and pace, you're going to have to vary your distance to the target, from perhaps three feet all the way back to forty feet. Especially if you're by yourself and using several balls, you're going to have a hard time putting each one to make it, and you're not going to see the ball go in the hole as often as you should when you practice.

That's why I recommend the drill Bill Shean used, putting to the fringe. If you don't like that, stick a tee in the turf and putt to it. That will simulate practicing for touch the way the pros do on the days before a tournament starts. They putt to tees or to small dots painted on the grass by the superintendent, signifying where the cups are going to be during the tournament.

But I don't see good players spending a lot of practice time working on pace and longer putts, whether it's to the fringe or to a tee, or to a spot painted on the grass. They do it just enough to get a feel for the greens they're playing in a given tournament.

Some players find it hard to get confident unless they feel they've practiced to make sure their alignment is good—that their putter blade is perpendicular to the target line, that their eyes are over the ball, their shoulders are square, etc. These matters all fall under the heading of putting mechanics. If you want to practice them, in my opinion the best place to do so is at home. Find a rug with a straight edge or a straight line in its design. Practice your stroke up and down this line all you like. Use a mirror to check your posture. But do all these things without a golf ball. Remember that when you practice with a ball and a hole, you're practicing putting to make it, not putting to check your alignment or your putter path.

If you want a drill that allows you to use a ball, a club, and a hole, and at the same time indirectly check your alignment, try the chalk line drill. It's the best putting practice tool I know of. There are lots of putting gadgets on the market, all claiming to be the answer to your putting woes and all priced as if they were. For my money, the best practice aid isn't sold through infomercials and isn't carried in golf shops. Nor will you find it advertised in golf magazines. It's in the hardware store, and it costs ten or fifteen dollars. It's the chalk line.

This is a tool that builders use to put lines on the ground to guide them in digging. It's basically a reel of string encased in a plastic shell that includes blue chalk dust.

To work on your putting with a chalk line, find a straight putt of about ten feet on your practice green. Shake the reel to coat the string with chalk dust. Then let out about ten feet of string. Pin one end of the string with a tee or a pencil to your hole. Let the string run along the straight putting line you've selected. Pull it taut and then snap it against the ground. It will leave a faint blue line on the ground. (It's harmless to the turf, by the way.)

Now all you need to do is center a ball on the line and putt it into the hole. You'll be amazed at how often it goes in. Using a chalk line, you can effortlessly sink putt after putt from eight or ten feet.

There's only one way you can mess up the chalk line drill, and that's by consciously trying to steer your putter along the line on the ground. That defeats the purpose. I don't know precisely what the magic of the chalk line is. I only know that the visual aid of the line will allow you to adjust your alignment and your putter blade subconsciously until everything is square. It will enhance your ability to roll the putt precisely along the line to the hole. Of course, you'll have complete trust in that line, because you'll already know that the putt is straight.

I know many pros who work regularly with a chalk line when they're at home, polishing their games before a tournament. I'm sure I'd see it more often on Tour, but some of the superintendents at Tour courses try to discourage its use. They know that once someone lays a chalk line down on the practice green, nearly every golfer in the field is going to want to use it, and they'll get too much wear in that portion of the practice green.

Presumably, though, the superintendent at your course won't have that problem. That's because only a small fraction of the players at most clubs systematically practice putting and even fewer understand the value of the chalk line.

There's only one pitfall with chalk line practice. It works so well that some players get overly fond of it. They stop practicing short putts without the chalk line. Then, in competition, they find themselves missing the chalk line, doubting their ability to putt without it. So use it in conjunction with other putting practice. Over time, you'll find that you will start to "see" a line away from the practice green. That's part of the magic of the chalk line.

I LIKE TO see players turn putting practice into a game. If you've got a friend on the practice green with you, for instance, you might want to try a little variation on the drill of putting to the fringe. The players start at the same point and putt to the same area of fringe. The player closest to the edge gets a point. If he stops his ball precisely on the edge, he gets two points. Points can be translated into nickels, dimes, and quarters if you like to have a small bet going. This kind of game enhances your interest in practice and helps you practice putting under a little pressure.

I'll even relax my rule against practicing longer putts toward a hole if it's part of a game. Brad Faxon, Billy Andrade, and Davis Love III often play a putting green practice game they call "Look and Shoot." Two players find a couple of holes about fifteen feet apart. Each player takes one ball. You putt your ball toward the other guy's hole, trying to make it, and vice versa. There's no time to read the green or take a practice stroke. Each time a player holes his putt, the contestants switch holes. If they miss, they putt the balls back and forth till someone makes one. They keep at it till someone has made five putts.

When it's done properly, the pace of this drill is very brisk. The competing players keep one another from getting too careful. They make sure the opponent has time only to look at the target and react to it. It makes them both putt very athletically.

At the clubs I visit, I've seen countless variations of another game. Everyone in this contest putts toward a hole perhaps thirty feet away. If someone gets the ball in the hole, he instantly wins two units from everyone else in the game. The player whose first putt is farthest from the hole has a choice. He can either attempt his second putt or pass on it. If he passes, he loses one unit to everyone. If he tries and misses, he loses two units to everyone. If he tries and makes it, there's no blood. The loser chooses the next putt and the game starts again.

This is a good practice game because it puts a premium on getting the ball into the hole. It introduces competitive pressure. And if you've got four or five buddies jingling change and making unhelpful remarks about your putting stroke when you line up a four-footer, it helps to develop a routine that insulates you from distractions and pressure.

This kind of game will help you find the seemingly paradoxical place where most good putters' minds reside. They hit practice putts as if they were in a tournament, and they hit tournament putts as if they were practicing.

That is, when they practice, good putters employ their mental routines. They putt to make every putt that involves a hole. Then, when they're in competition, the practice they've put in helps them relax, focus on the target, and stroke their putts freely.

That's effective practice.

A ·Word About Wedges

Improve your chipping and you automatically improve your scoring.

—Tom Watson

What's a chapter on wedge play doing in a book about putting?

Try a little experiment. Next time you're on a practice green, drop five balls ten feet from a hole. Putt them, putting to make each of them. Count the number that fall. Now take the same five balls and drop them three feet from the hole. Make it hard on yourself. Use the leading edge of your sand wedge to putt them.

I'll bet that more balls go in off the edge of the sand wedge from three feet than drop from ten feet using a proper putter.

And that's why, even though this is a book about putting, I want to say a little bit about wedge play. Give me the average hacker from three feet and you can have Loren Roberts or Brad

Faxon or Ben Crenshaw from ten feet. Despite their considerable skills, they're going to miss more from ten feet than a poor putter will miss from three feet.

Good wedge play makes the difference between a lot of putts from ten feet and a lot of putts from three feet. If you knock your chips and pitches closer to the hole, you're going to make more putts.

Wedge play is one reason why putting statistics don't always show who's the best putter. The statistics count the average number of putts a player makes on greens he's hit in regulation. What they don't reflect is the average length of those putts. A player with mediocre wedge games may be leaving his pitches twenty feet from the hole on short par-4s and on par-5s, both the sorts of holes where a good player is likely to have an approach to the green from about one hundred yards. A player with a better wedge game may be leaving himself an average of ten feet from the hole in those situations. Consequently, he makes more putts.

Good wedge play belongs in that category of fundamental skills I've mentioned already, skills analogous to playing good defense and rebounding in basketball. Just as winning basketball teams make it a priority to play defense and rebound, winning golfers make it a priority to hit their wedges close to, or in the hole.

I've seen improved wedge play elevate a professional's game. It can be the difference between playing on the Buy.com Tour and playing, and winning, on the PGA Tour.

Michael Clark II and I started working together years ago,

when he was playing at Georgia Tech. Mike had a lot of talent. But, as he would be the first to tell you, he didn't have a lot of maturity, or a lot of luck. He didn't practice as much as he should have in college. He didn't play as well as he should have.

When he turned pro, he had a series of injuries. They kept him from climbing the ladder quickly. But they also helped Mike discover persistence, strength of will, and purpose. He kept plugging away at the game, even when the rewards were scant.

As he matured, Mike began to realize that his wedge game was one of the things keeping him from being the player he wanted to be. He was capable of shooting low scores when his swing was in synch. But he wasn't able to use his wedges and chips to prevent a 75 or 76 on days when his swing wasn't working as well.

For Mike, the key to improving his wedge game was unleashing his creativity. He had been taught as a boy to hit a lot of bump-and-run shots. They were the shots he felt most comfortable with, the shots he instinctively wanted to hit in most situations around the green. But in professional golf, the fashion was for high wedge shots. Mike became, in a sense, a victim of fashion. He found himself torn in many situations between the creative bump-and-run shot his instincts told him to hit and the high, fly-it-to-the-hole-and-stop-it shot his peers tended to hit. Indecision, of course, is as fatal in the wedge game as it is in putting.

Gradually, over the past couple of years, Mike found a solution. He started to rely more on the sorts of bump-and-run shots he loved to play as a boy. But he also worked hard on his soft, high wedges, especially from bunkers, so he'd have them when he needed them.

When he went to the Tour qualifying school last year, Mike found that his swing was not where he wanted it to be. He wasn't hitting it too well. But his wedge game saved him. On one of the first holes of the first round, he found himself with a tough little shot to play—over about ten feet of Bermuda rough and then over about fifteen feet of green to the hole. It was slightly uphill. He hesitated. His instinct told him to hit a nine-iron and try to chip it in. He had a second thought, which was a safe wedge into the slope. Mike this time went with his instinct and hit an excellent chip, landing it in the fringe and running it up to the hole. It lipped out, leaving him a tap-in par putt. His confidence got an enormous boost from the knowledge that even with his swing out of whack, he could still score.

Despite having a kinky swing the first three days, Mike managed to shoot 66, 68, and 70. Then he got his swing straightened out, thanks to a tip from his old college coach, Puggy Blackmon. He shot a 63 in the fourth round. He eventually finished eleventh at the school and got his card for the PGA Tour. In his rookie season he won the John Deere Classic and established himself as a player to be reckoned with. And the primary difference in his game was his wedge play and, not coincidentally, his putting.

• • •

It's not my purpose here to discuss the mechanics of the various chips and pitches a good golfer must be able to hit. If you have a problem with your short-game mechanics, see a pro, settle on a method, and stick to it.

But I do want to point out some of the ways in which a sound mental routine for wedge play resembles a sound mental routine for putting.

The first and most important is that good chippers and pitchers always try to hole their shots from within a threshold distance, just as good putters always putt to make it. They're not thinking about getting it close or leaving themselves an uphill putt. They're thinking about holing the shot.

Second, the chipping and pitching routine of good players resembles the putting routine at its core. They look at the target, look at the ball, and let the shot go. It's athletic, creative, almost improvisational. Think of a basketball player pulling up and shooting the open jumper in the split second before his defender can adjust. Think of a third baseman scooping up a bunt with his bare hand and throwing on the run toward the outstretched glove at first base. At the critical moment, these athletes simply react to the target without thinking. So does a good wedge player.

Mike Clark told me about a shot he was particularly proud of at the qualifying school. It came in the final round. He'd hit the ball over the green with his second shot on the par-5 16th hole.

He had a delicate pitch back up a slope, a shot he'd have to play like an explosion from the Bermuda rough. Mike simply went through his routine. And at its climax, he started taking the club back as soon as his eyes returned to the ball after his final look at the target. There was no hesitation. He knocked it four feet from the hole.

If you react similarly to your target, you'll be well on your way to solving one of the common problems in wedge play, a problem very similar to the problem of speed in putting. With a wedge, the issue is how far to hit the ball. Many golfers find it's not too hard to chip the ball toward their target. But they tie themselves up trying to make sure they chip it the right distance.

Some years ago, I worked with a pro named Buddy Harston from Lexington Country Club in Lexington, Kentucky. Buddy was unhappy about several aspects of his game, particularly wedge play. I took a look at Buddy's routine. There was a long gap between his last look at the target and the beginning of his swing. I asked him what he was doing during that interval.

Buddy told me he was trying to visualize the shot he was about to hit, starting with the swing he intended to make and finishing with the ball rolling close to the hole.

I told him that the time to visualize was when he was standing behind the ball, planning his shot, not when he was about to execute it. At the core of his routine, I wanted him to look at the target and let the shot go within seconds.

I knew Buddy had been a baseball player in his youth. He

played second base on some teams that reached the College World Series. I asked him how he'd handled the cut-off play responsibilities of a second baseman.

"I went out into the outfield and put my hands up and caught the ball and listened for the shortstop to tell me where to throw," Buddy said. "Then I whirled and threw it there."

"You didn't stop and visualize how you were going to throw it?" I asked.

Buddy understood. "No, of course not. There wasn't time. I just threw it where the shortstop told me to."

"And it went the right distance?"

"Yes."

That, I told him, was how his wedge game would work best, too. I wanted him to get set up, take a last look at the target, and let the shot go without delay. His athletic ability would make sure the ball went the right distance, so long as he was reacting to that target.

Buddy tried it and the results were dramatic. He soon won his first significant championship as a professional, a section PGA competition in Kentucky. He's won many more since then. Today, he's looking forward to a chance to qualify for the Senior PGA tour.

He might make it if he keeps reacting to his target with his wedges and his putter.

There are a couple of nuances in wedge play that differ from putting. The first is the selection of a target during the preshot routine. Some players like to home in on the cup just as they do in putting. They use the cup as a target on straight chips and pitches. They pick out an imaginary target to the left or right of the cup on shots that will break.

Others envision their shot and see a point on the green where they want the ball to land. They imagine a specific trajectory for the airborne portion of the shot. They foresee how the ball will roll once it lands. So when they chip or pitch, their target is a spot on the green that might be a long way from the hole.

It doesn't matter which way you prefer to do it. If you're not already a confirmed believer in one way or the other, experiment around the practice green. Choose the method that appeals more to you and stick with it.

The second nuance involves your threshold distance. That's the distance within which you always try to hole a shot. You try to make every putt. But you try to hole only those wedges that are played from within your threshold distance. For Tour pros, who wouldn't be where they are without precise control of their wedges, the threshold distance might be 120 yards, which is the distance a professional generally hits a wedge. Whenever he has a shot from that distance or less, he should be thinking about holing it.

For amateurs, whose control is less precise, the threshold distance may be shorter—twenty, thirty, sixty yards. And there may be occasions when you have to adjust it. Suppose, for instance, that you have twenty yards to the green and the hole is cut five yards from the front edge. Your normal threshold distance is fifty yards. In that situation, you might normally be thinking of pitching the ball to the edge of the green and letting it roll in. But let's add a pond to the situation—beginning just in front of you and extending to the very edge of the green. Your wedge control may not be precise enough for you to risk trying to land the ball a couple of feet beyond the water. You may have to aim for a spot deeper on the green and settle for a shot that leaves you beyond the hole, but dry. Such situations, though, are relatively rare. Most of the time, when inside your threshold distance, think about holing it.

And then practice it. While it's possible to be a good putter without spending too much time practicing putting, I don't know many good wedge players who don't work constantly to keep that aspect of their game sharp. They've fallen in love with getting the ball up and down, or chipping it in, and they like practicing it. It's quite common for pros on the Tour to spend an hour and a half every day practicing around the greens.

There's no mystery to how to do this. Walk ten paces out from the edge of your practice green. Circle the green using the new radius you've established. Everything within this circle is your practice area. Within it, you'll find, I hope, a rich variety of short-game situations—tight lies and grassy lies, side slopes and humps, chips and pitches. There should be a practice bunker somewhere within this circle for sand shots. If not, you can always wait till twilight or early morning and use a bunker on the course.

Let your imagination work as you practice. Try a variety of

ways to put the ball in a hole from a given situation. Lob it close, then chip it and let it run to the hole. You'll sharpen both your touch and your sense of what shot best fits a given situation.

If you're a high-handicap player, your wedge game by definition isn't as sharp as a pro's. If it were, you wouldn't have a high handicap. Your practice can help you address some of the common problems that less skilled players have with the short game.

Many amateurs, I know, worry about skulling or chilidipping their short shots, particularly from tight lies. The best cure for this is practicing from bare dirt. If you practice on a range, it's not hard to find a spot where the grass has been hacked away by someone else. (If you don't practice on a range with grass tees, but you play a lot of golf, it's likely that the grass in your backyard isn't all that lush. That's because you're probably out on the course when you could be laying down fertilizer. Now you can reap a benefit from neglecting your yard. You can find a bare spot there and use it for short-game practice.) Wherever you do it, learn to hit from bare dirt. When you encounter a tight lie on the golf course, it'll seem easy by comparison.

You may be wondering, now that I've suggested practice drills and games for your putting, and I've suggested lots of practice for your short game, when do I expect you to work on your cherished goal of learning to hit a precisely faded seven-iron to a tight pin?

The answer is that I don't. If you're a tournament pro whose business is playing golf, you might have time to work on that sort of shot. But if you make your living off the golf course, you probably don't. Part-time golfers whose practice time is limited ought to spend nearly all of it on three areas—putting, the short game, and whatever club—driver or fairway wood—they rely on for most tee shots.

Until you become proficient from all lies with your wedges, there's nothing wrong with using a putter from tight lies, where that's possible. I've seen some players have good results using the three-wood from the fringe, rather than hitting a traditional chip. That's fine, too. The Scots invented golf, and they use putters anywhere within forty yards of the green.

But you will not be playing your best golf until your wedge game is sharp enough that bad lies don't deter you, until no matter where you find yourself around a green, you have a chip or a pitch that you feel you can put in the hole.

When you reach that level, you'll need fewer putts.

How You'll Putt from Now On

I've always been a good putter and I probably always will be.

—TOM KITE

NOW YOU KNOW WHAT IT TAKES TO BE A GOOD PUTTER. THE QUEStion is, how will you apply what you know? What kind of commitment are you prepared to make to it?

I sometimes run into people who have read one of my earlier books, most notably *Golf Is Not a Game of Perfect*. And sometimes one of these readers will say, "The stuff in that book worked great for a while, Doc. I was really playing well. But it doesn't work so well anymore."

When I have a chance to talk with one of these people, it becomes clear that the stuff in the book isn't the problem. Commitment to it is the problem. When the book was fresh in their minds, they trusted their swings, they managed their golf games intelligently, they disposed of anger on the course. They did a lot of things right and their scores showed it. But with time, their old habits of thought reasserted themselves. They started to think about their swing mechanics when they played, and to try to fix them. They started to make foolish strategy choices. They started to let anger affect their next shots. And their scores went up as a result.

Thus the question: How will you apply what you now know about putting? What sort of commitment will you make to it?

The principles of putting in this book will work, but only if you apply them for an extended period of time—say, six months to a year. And they'll continue to work for as long as your commitment stands. They'll stop working if your commitment fades.

Don't think that keeping a commitment to these ideas will be easy. Making a commitment is easy. Keeping it is hard. That's because no system, no set of ideas, will turn you into a putting wizard. Putting isn't wizardry. It's an art, and there are days when it's a capricious art. There are going to be times when you miss putts you think you should have made. There are going to be times when those missed putts will cost you a match or a title you dearly wanted to win.

That's when keeping a commitment begins to get hard. That's when other paths will become tempting. There are always going to be people in the golf world trying to persuade you that their grip, or their putter, or their practice aid, or their stroke is the answer. There are always going to be people telling you that there's no point in trying to be a good putter because you have no talent and it's an impossible, unjust part of the game anyway. If you listen to them, you won't keep your commitment.

If you want to keep your commitment, it will help if you know you're committed to a process, a process that works. The process isn't dependent on how many putts you take on a given hole or round. Those numbers will fluctuate, though the trend will be downward.

If you're the sort of player who adds up his putts at the end of a round and evaluates himself by the number he made, the number of three-putts or whatever, you may need a new way of thinking to buttress your commitment. Instead of asking, How many times did I putt this round?, you need to ask, How many times did I putt without executing my mental routine? How many times did I fail to simply see it and do it? If the answer is never, then the number of putts you actually took is irrelevant (though it will usually be satisfyingly low).

If you'd like to keep a commitment to change the way you putt, you might do well to have some criteria by which you can monitor the way you're thinking. Here are some ideas that might help you:

Do you love putting on whatever sort of green you encounter, fast or slow, grainy or smooth?

Do you welcome the challenge of putting?

Do you take pride in how free and confident you are with your putter?

Do you execute your mental and physical routine on every putt?

Do you refuse to let missed putts bother you? Do you stick with your routine and habits of mind even when putts don't fall on the first nine holes?

Do you always putt to make it?

Do you ever permit your fear of three-putting to dominate your love of one-putting?

When you talk about your putting to others, do you talk about how well you're putting rather than whine or complain?

Do you try to recall the great putts you've made and forget the ones you've missed?

If you're coming up with the wrong answers to those questions, then it's time to reexamine and reinvigorate your commitment.

Don't think of this commitment as a porcelain vase that, once broken, can never be put together again. I don't know of any player whose mind is always where it ought to be. Every player I've ever worked with has had occasions when he's putted in fear or doubt, when he's tried to steer the ball into the hole. Good players recognize when their commitments waver, and they set things right quickly. They constantly recommit themselves.

But while keeping your commitment to good putting won't be easy, neither will it be like keeping a commitment to go to the dentist twice a year. Putting well is fun.

You're going to love the difference thinking well about putting makes in your golf game.

If we could turn that theoretical computer-assisted mind-scanning device I spoke of earlier onto the mind of a good putter, we'd find these kinds of pleasant thoughts:

All right! Safely on the green. Now the fun starts. This is going to be an interesting putt. I can see two breaks. Downhill. A real challenge. Neat! I like the fact that my partner has no doubts that I'm going to make par or better on this hole. I like being the bulwark of our team because I putt well. I like the way the other guys' faces will look when I sink this for a birdie. Okay, now into the routine. . . .

You're going to love knowing that the way you putt and think about putting gives you a big advantage over the rest of the players in your weekly foursome, the ones who are always grumbling about putting and buying new putters. You're going to love seeing a three-foot putt for par and knowing you'll make it. You're going to love being the guy who rescues holes given up for lost with a great putt. You're going to love watching your golf ball roll firmly and boldly across a green full of treacherous waves and currents, and then drop toward the hole like a sailboat making for harbor. You're going to love that moment of clarity, when confusion burns away like a morning fog and you see the line your ball must follow. You're going to love the sound of the ball rattling in the hole.

You're going to love to putt.

Appendix

1. No matter how skilled you are with the long clubs, you're going to make roughly 40 percent of your shots with your putter.
2. The putting game is the place to look if you want to get a competitive advantage.
3. The ideal golf temperament instinctively loves putting.
4. In putting, the inability to forget is infinitely more devastating than the inability to remember. There's nothing worse for your putting than dwelling on the putts you've missed.
5. Thinking the way you have always thought will almost certainly assure that you putt the way you have always putted.

6. You'll make your best stroke and hole the most putts if you think only of your target.

7. Orientation toward the target works because the subconscious brain is capable of quick, accurate adjustments.

8. The smaller the target you have, the better the brain and body can function in getting the ball there.

9. Never putt for a three-foot circle. If you aren't trying to hole every putt you have, you are going to lose to someone who is.

10. To gain control, give up control.

11. Devotion to an unvarying routine is one of the hallmarks of a good putter.

12. When the moment of truth comes, look at the target, look at the ball, and let the stroke go without any undue delay between these three movements.

13. Your first impression of how a putt will break will be right more often than any other impression you might form.

14. Putt to make it.

15. More often than not, anger is the enemy of focus.

16. Good players handle pressure putts by developing a strong routine and relying on it in the clutch.

17. Good putters learn to welcome nervous symptoms rather than fear them.

18. The last thing you want to do if you're trying to make putts is worry about speed.

19. You already have touch. You have to believe in it and use it.

20. A miss is a miss, whether it runs a foot past the hole or stops a foot short.

21. Every putt is a green-light putt.

22. The yips originate in the mind. Their prevention and cure are mental challenges.

23. If you think the putter you're using will help you, it probably will.

24. Pick a putter and a putting style that feel good to you and stick with them.

25. There is no such thing as perfect putting mechanics. There is no perfect way to roll the ball.

26. Fall in love with the stroke you have.

27. Practice in ways that build confidence.

28. Practicing for touch and pace is best done without a hole.

29. Good wedge play makes the difference between a lot of putts from ten feet and a lot of putts from three feet.

30. The principles of good putting will work for as long as your commitment to them stands.